PRAISE FOR

CRISIS EVANGELISM

Few people are so well qualified to write a book of such significance for our time. This is a message for every believer.

DR. BILL BRIGHT

Founder and President,
Campus Crusade for Christ International
Orlando, Florida

For many years, Drs. Mark and Betsy Neuenschwander have steadfastly served hurting humanity, ministering life in the midst of disaster. They are not alarmists, but they know that when people are in trouble, Christians can demonstrate Christ's love with remarkable effectiveness. That's what this book is all about. This call for preparation isn't a scare tactic—it is a timely and godly push toward readiness so we can effectively communicate His love to others.

TED HAGGARD

Senior Pastor, New Life Church
Colorado Springs, Colorado

Praise God for this practical, balanced, no-fear-mongering resource for addressing a perplexing current issue.

JACK HAYFORD

Senior Pastor, The Church On The Way
Van Nuys, California

It's time for the Church to get salty so the lost will thirst for the Living Water. The Neuenschwanders have written a challenging book that will encourage the Body of Christ to be like Jesus. I highly recommend it.

CINDY JACOBS

Cofounder, Generals of Intercession
Colorado Springs, Colorado

CRISIS EVANGELISM

Preparing to be
Salt and Light
When the World
Needs Us Most

CRISIS
EVANGELISM

MARK NEUENSCHWANDER, M.D.
BETSY NEUENSCHWANDER, M.D.

Regal

A Division of Gospel Light
Ventura, California, U.S.A.

Published by Regal Books
A Division of Gospel Light
Ventura, California, U.S.A.
Printed in U.S.A.

Cover Design by Kevin Keller
Interior Design by Rob Williams
Edited by Ron Durham and Deena Davis

Library of Congress Cataloging-in-Publication Data
Neuenschwander, Mark, 1949–
    Crisis evangelism / by Mark and Betsy Neuenschwander.
        p.   cm.
    Includes bibliographical references.
    ISBN 0-8307-2490-7 (trade)
    1. Evangelistic work. 2. Crisis management—Religious aspects— Christianity.
    I. Neuenschwander, Betsy, 1948–   . II. Title
    BV3793.N48   1999   99-20546
    269'.2—dc21   CIP

01 02 03 04 05 06 07 08 09 10 11 12 13 14 15 / 05 04 03 02 01 00 99

Rights for publishing this book in other languages are contracted by Gospel Literature International (GLINT). GLINT also provides technical help for the adaptation, translation and publishing of Bible study resources and books in scores of languages worldwide. For further information, contact GLINT, P.O. Box 4060, Ontario, CA 91761-1003, U.S.A. You may also send E-mail to Glintint@aol.com, or visit their website at www.glint.org.

Dedicated to the heart of Jesus—
that none should perish!

CONTENTS

FOREWORD

Every tragedy has two faces. The first is the face of the Great Destroyer, seen in such atrocities as "ethnic cleansing" in the Balkans, the bombing of the Murrah Federal Building in Oklahoma City, the tears and trauma of rape victims in Indonesia.

The second face is quieter but infinitely more powerful. It is our heavenly Father's light-filled, tender countenance that shines into the darkest of places through the active love and compassion of the saints. God's face is toward those who suffer. As we follow His gaze, we are not only moved with compassion, we see where our heavenly Father is working, and we join Him. As we become "salt and light," God takes that which the enemy intended for evil and uses it mightily for His Kingdom purposes. He energizes the Body of Christ and reaches the lost.

There will always be battlefields and refugees, but food and medical aid brought life and comfort to thousands in Kosovo. As Oklahoma City picked up the pieces, pastors were given both positions of leadership and unprecedented platforms to reach the nation. And violence in Indonesia—one of the most staunchly Muslim countries in the world—has spurred unprecedented thousands of people to their knees, leading them to the true security found only in Jesus Christ.

For many years, Drs. Mark and Betsy Neuenschwander have observed the truth of God's redemption, and they have lived it. God has wielded them like a sword of light to penetrate the darkest camps of the enemy, bringing both physical and spiritual food to starving and shattered people from North Korea to Yugoslavia to Rwanda. And now the Lord has brought them back to the United States to prepare the American Church for what may be an unusually great time of need...and of opportunity.

As we face the uncertainties of the months and years ahead, the Neuenschwanders are uniquely qualified to show the Body of Christ how to minister to others during any type of crisis. Whether for the unexpected tragedy of a natural disaster, or the foreseeable pain of a Y2K economic downturn, *Crisis Evangelism* beautifully conveys the heart of God toward the needy and lost, and it spurs the Christian toward practical responses that meet the needs of both the body and soul of those who are in crisis.

No one but God can know exactly what lies in front of us. The only thing we can know for sure is that we are to permeate and illuminate this dark world with the love and truth of Jesus Christ, in whatever situations we find ourselves. In time of trouble, God has given us a specific promise and a challenge: "So will I save you, and you will be a blessing. Do not be afraid, but let your hands be strong" (Zech. 8:13).

Make it so, Lord.

Shaunti Christine Feldhahn
Author, *Y2K: The Millennium Bug: A Balanced Christian Response*

ACKNOWLEDGMENTS

With deep gratitude we would like to thank those especially strategic in the composition of this book. First, to Rev. Retha Garten, president of Northern Florida Christian Center, who has nurtured and pastored us personally for the last 22 years. We are thankful for Beverly Pegues, director of Christian Information Network, who first prophesied this book's inception. Loving credit to Quin Sherrer, who catalyzed our friendship with Regal Books. Appreciation goes to Carol Ruddick who launched the logistics. Roaring and heartfelt applause to June Lewis who suffered and persevered, helping us with the initial text. Dr. Bob and Mrs. Leslie Walden were also of great help in emergency preparedness by helping speed-type and proofing some of the chapters. Warm thanks to Dr. Ron Durham, our editor, for his patience, flexibility and assistance. We offer voluminous indebtedness to Bob Stroud, who "nursed along" the whole project technologically, with great deskside manner. Profuse thanks to our contributing authors, Nancy Stroud and Don Larson, for their expertise.

All of the above were bathed in regular prayer by our Monday night prayer regulars, Wand Elliot's Tuesday morning intercessors, Barry Daniels, and the 6:00 A.M. New Life spiritual warriors, plus our prayer support in Malaysia, South Korea, and India!

To God be the glory—great things *He* has done!

†

INTRODUCTION
FROM OUR HEARTS TO YOURS

We felt a kinship with you as we wrote this book, knowing your similar concerns for the future of our country and world. We count it a privilege to share with you. It is exciting to us that Christians are called by Jesus to be salt and light on the earth, particularly in light of the currently increasing number of crises and disasters which, of course, Scripture assures us are signs that we are living in the last days!

Our exhortation to you to become totally committed in responding to God's call by serving others in dire situations is neither naïve nor something we have not personally experienced. We know firsthand the sacrifice it requires. Leaving the security, affluence and comfort of the United States 13 years ago, to minister full-time in India, Bangladesh, Pakistan, Nepal and other countries of Asia was neither easy nor comfortable.

We trained many years, preparing to reach out to the world's destitute—Dr. Mark nine years after medical school and Dr. Betsy seven years. Each of us worked 80 to 100 hours a week for 10 years. I (Dr. Mark) completed board certification in General Surgery and Family Practice, and Dr. Betsy is board certified as an OB/GYN, as well as in Family Practice.

Our specific intention during this arduous training was to become medical missionaries. One of my (Dr. Mark's) earliest memories is tugging on my Catholic mother's apron strings and saying, "Mom, I want to be a missionary priest!" Today on the wall in our home is a picture of Dr. Betsy at age five, outfitted in pretend surgical garb with Dad's white handkerchiefs covering her head and mouth as she operates on her doll who had lost its arm. She certainly had a head start on trauma surgery! Our heart, however, is not just to heal physical needs of suffering millions. We also long to bring eternal rescue, because the greatest disaster is one that lasts forever—the loss of eternal life.

We left the United States in raw obedience to be doers of Matthew 28:19,20, the Great Commission, and not hearers only. We landed in Calcutta, India, on December 27, 1986, having left lucrative medical practices, resigned medical school faculty positions and sold most of our possessions. Suddenly stripped of the comforts of electricity, running water, heating and air-conditioning, we were able to identify immediately with the physical suffering around us. Soon we began to feel the spiritual needs of the people as well. Walking through Calcutta's Howrah train station, stumbling over wall-to-wall people lying on pallets, stepping over dead bodies left in the streets—all this forever broke our hearts. Indeed "Christ's love compels us, because we are convinced . . . he died for all, that those who live should no longer live for themselves but for him who died for them and was raised again" (2 Cor. 5:14,5).

During the last twelve and one-half years we have ministered in 41 nations, holding evangelistic and healing crusades, teaching Rural Health Care courses to Bible school students (400 graduates) and conducting Spiritual Warfare Institutes for professionals (1,800 graduates). Convinced that it is better to teach people "how to fish" than to just "give them a fish," our focus has been to train indigenous professionals—engineers, dentists, Christian workers, nurses, builders, pastors, physicians, computer specialists, paramedics, evangelists—to effectively "fish for men" and then train others. We give God the glory as He has used our medical credentials and commitment to professionalism to open many doors with governmental officials, including Ministers of Health.

In 1995, because people often come to Christ during times of crisis, God expanded our evangelism-training repertoire by launching Disaster Response Schools. These schools targeted the mammoth crisis scenarios among Hindus, Muslims and Buddhists of the 10/40 Window—the latitudes between which most of the unreached peoples live, in 62 nations. An opportunity for which we are most grateful was when our faculty conducted disaster training for the Ministry of Health in Taiwan, attended by 153 government officials—at which we expounded the gospel three times. Similar schools have also been conducted for Christians in South Korea, Malaysia, India and the United States. In addition, in 1998, our organization served almost 2 million meals in areas of the 10/40 Window devastated by famine.

PREPARING FOR THE TIMES AHEAD

As Dr. Betsy and I were submitting the final edits of our book to our publisher, we attended, with over 2,700 other people, a strategic conference hosted by the Wagner Institute in Colorado Springs, from January 28 to January 30, 1999. This conference was the National School of the Prophets' "Mobilizing the Prophetic Office of the Next Century." The day before this conference convened, there was a first-time gathering of several elder prophets of national stature, representing various streams of the Church, for the express purpose of seeking the Lord as to what He is saying to His Church in the United States of America. Some of the prophets and leaders assembled included Paul Cain, Rick Joyner, Cindy Jacobs, Bill Hamon, John and Paula Sandford, Chuck Pierce, Jim Laffoon, Kinsgley Fletcher, Jim Gall, Barbara Wentroble, Hector Torres, Mike Bickle and Dutch Sheets.

Believing that God still speaks through His prophets today, we are admonished to listen to what is spoken: "Surely the Lord God does nothing unless He reveals His secret counsel to His servants the prophets" (Amos 3:7, *NASB*). "The secret things belong to the LORD our God, but the things revealed belong to us and to our sons forever" (Deut. 29:29, *NASB*). As you read this partial summation of the words spoken on January 27, 1999, please remember that personal and national prophecy is conditional—there must be enough godly sorrow and genuine repentance, with people turning from their evil deeds.

A PROPHETIC WORD FOR AMERICA

PREPARATION

What is coming upon the world is so serious that Y2K will pale in comparison. It is all right to prepare in the natural, provided that the preparation is not a heaping up solely for our own personal needs, without considering the plight of neighbors. If storing is done selfishly, it will be like sifting sand, and slip through our fingers.

The Church is not to fall into fear and panic, but to seek His face and presence. We each need to prepare spiritually, both individually and regionally, for what lies ahead. This is done in intercession through establishing the "Watch of the Lord" with 24-hour prayer and praise. We must rebuild the walls of our cities like Nehemiah, establishing the 12 gates of prayer and praise.

INTERNATIONAL ALLIANCES

By witness of several prophetic voices, it is believed that an alliance will form between Communism and Islam, creating an evil that will be more difficult than anything we have previously known in modern history. Europe particularly needs to cry to the Lord. If Europeans cry out with all their hearts, God will hear them in their day of trouble. American intercessors in particular are to be of great help to them in that time. A word came that war is coming and that many of our own young men and women will die on this soil and foreign soil if we do not cry out to God.

TERRORISM

The accuser of the brethren is coming with a fresh onslaught. There will be Islamic terrorist attacks that will be launched against children, and will put tremendous fear and even terror into the heart of the nation. This fear could boomerang, especially against those who are in militia organizations and certain groups of Christians. As a result, a wave of persecution could come against the Church.

ECONOMIC SHAKINGS

The Lord spoke strongly of economic shakings to come. Several dreams have been given to various prophets about disaster striking the nation, in particular the East Coast. The Lord was showing that we are not ready in any measure for what is coming, and that it will be titanic in proportion when it hits in its fullness.

One of His last words in our assembly was that because of our prayers and standing in the gap (it seems this meant because of the tears and deep intercession of God's people worldwide) that complete destruction will be averted. In the coming shakings, so many things will be happening that those in the Church who have been against spiritual warfare are going to be awakened and realize their great need, and stand up and fight against the enemy in that day.

DAYS OF GLORY

If the Church will arise [now] and lay hold of this window of opportunity that lies in front of us, the days of hardship could be turned into days of great hope. It is a time for humility; a time for intercession; a time for spiritual and natural preparation; and a time for God's glory to shine forth and let light overcome darkness. There is coming a wave of God's great glory that will supersede anything we have seen in recent Church history. The call is for us to shake off our apathy, arise as a beacon of light, and through prayer and compassionate deeds of the saints, seize the moment while we still can.

SALT AND LIGHT IN CRUCIAL TIMES

In the light of this word for America, do we need to heed these warnings and seek diligently the face of God for His plan and strategy, not only for our families and loved ones, but also for our churches and communities? Is it possible for us to believe that our Lord, who sees ahead, would be pleased for us to believe Him for the resources and strategies of provisions for the elderly, the disabled, and single-parent families who may lack the resources to fend for themselves? We know from history that the Marshall Plan was powerfully used to feed and sustain Europe after World War II. Would the Holy Spirit want you to help raise up a preemptive Marshall Plan in your church and community? This book will help move you in the right direction to carry this out!

We (Dr. Mark and Dr. Betsy) believe that God has temporarily assigned us as veteran missionaries back home to help prepare the American Church to stand firm in crisis and disaster evangelism! Both of us are licensed, ordained and on the board of Victory

Fellowship of Ministries. We are also graduates of Victory World Mission Training Center, and of Youth With A Mission's Crossroads Discipleship School. We are also coordinators of AD 2000 and Beyond's Crisis Relief Task Force, and lead the United States Spiritual Warfare Task Force for Professionals under Dr. C. Peter Wagner and Cindy Jacobs.

We share this background with you in hopes that it will encourage your own participation as a minister of reconciliation in crucial times. We pray that when you turn the last page of this book and begin to practice its principles in your own community, you will have formed a spiritual alliance with us. It is our desire that each of us will continue to go from faith to faith and glory to glory in demonstrating the lordship of Jesus, His nature and character, so we can set the captives free!

Keep pressing toward the mark of the high calling!

—Drs. Mark and Betsy Neuenschwander

The Call to Prepare: Meeting Spiritual and Eternal Needs

The signs of our times are characterized in Matthew 24:7-14 by sudden but sometimes predictable disasters. "Cues" from Jesus Himself should be a wake-up call to Church leadership and a dress rehearsal for the Church to seize and enthusiastically live her finest hour of service and witness!

Jesus declared that Christians are the salt of the earth and the light of the world (Matt. 5:13-16). Today an unprecedented number of crisis situations throughout the world provide unique opportunities for us to be "sprinkled" salt, and to let our light shine as we relieve pain, demonstrate Jesus to the suffering and bring them to experience His glory.

Are you ready to be salt and light in the darkness of power outages, under dense, ominous storm clouds of war, amid natural disasters, in possible disruptions from "Y2K" computer problems and countless other calamitous events that engulf people with loss, despair and death? If Christians can offer not only the Savior Jesus, but also efficient and skilled emergency response, health care and ample supplies, then our faith will shine the light of hope for reconstructing victims' lives!

GOD'S HEART-CRY
BE SALT AND LIGHT

BETSY NEUENSCHWANDER, M.D.

Recall mental scenes of past disasters you have witnessed first-hand or viewed on CNN: people screaming in fear as buildings topple . . . scrambling for high ground away from rushing water or smoldering lava . . . crying out in pain because of crushed limbs, massive hemorrhaging, or in agony for their lost children, parents or spouses. Then, aid begins to trickle in. Ambulances arrive, firefighters control the flames, paramedics begin patching up the bodies.

SALT SPRINKLED

During those first moments of crisis, people's overriding motive is naturally self- and family-preservation. But Jesus declares that we Christians are the salt of the earth; so where Christians are present at a major crisis, the motive enlarges.

Salt (a Christian) is a preservative that retards decay. When the sprinkling of this "salt" begins, Christ's followers are observed seeking ways to preserve others! In times of chaos, it is so fulfilling to be a preserver, allowing God to sprinkle us into the situation as His Spirit's "sodium chloride," bringing healing and preservation.

Since Christians are to be love slaves to our Lord, our motivation should be like His, reaching beyond self-preservation (the survivalist mentality) to a deeper, more expansive ministry of blessing, helping and preserving those around us. Jesus mandates that we be salty—as in the days of Elisha:

> The men of the city said to Elisha, "Look . . . this town is well situated, as you can see, but the water is bad and the land is unproductive." "Bring me a new bowl," he said, "and put salt in it." . . . Then he went out to the spring and threw the salt into it, saying, "This is what the Lord says: 'I have healed this water. Never again will it cause death or make the land unproductive'" (2 Kings 2:19-21).

Depending upon the type of physical disaster—i.e., contaminated water, broken sewer lines, dispersed biological or chemical warfare agents—some type of purification will be needed for your area's water system. What if FEMA (the Federal Emergency Management Agency) and/or your local authorities are overwhelmed and can't provide response? If your church knew the scientific procedures for disaster relief, that knowledge would serve as Elisha's "salt." Further, if your congregation were prepared to act on that knowledge by blessing and serving the community in need, those very actions might, as salt, de-ice gospel-frozen hearts. Even further, if we minister the miraculous, as in 2 Kings 2, what an awesome preservative for soul and spirit we could be!

THE COST OF BEING SALTY

Salt is a clear, brittle mineral used to flavor, preserve and de-ice.

Chemically, salt is formed when a base completely neutralizes acid. Obtained by mining or evaporation, it is then crushed and ground.

Crushed? Yes, Christians must be willing to be "crushed" to become a better preserving force on the earth! Interestingly, the Hebrew word for salt, *melach*, actually means "easily pulverized and dissolved." The Greek word for salt in Matthew 5:13 is from *halas*, which figuratively means "prudence." Look at the spiritual significance of this in relation to crisis. Could calamitous experiences pulverize our own false foundations (believers and unbelievers alike), fracturing idols of self-trust, or primary trust in wealth, intelligence and talents, as well as shatter icons of comfort and security? Would, could, this force us to prudently choose greater intimacy and dependency upon Him? I think the persecuted Church of China, Pakistan, North Africa and others graphically demonstrates the intangible value of pulverization. In being crushed, these Christians have become salty savor indeed!

"But wait!" we scream. "Pulverizing hurts! Please, God, no! I'll sit on the back row and spectate. Listen—I hear the organ playing the altar call. What? What did he say? I can't believe he said, 'Please come forward, anyone who loves Jesus enough to surrender all for "pulverization" and "dissolving" to glorify our Lord!'"

Yet if we answer this call and let our values and priorities dissolve into our Father God's heart, then His agenda, His nature will emerge and He can sprinkle us into the gaping wounds of humanity's life crises. And, since salt de-ices, our servant presence in the midst of trauma or calamity can de-ice hearts that have been cold to the gospel!

Jesus warned that if the salt loses its "savor" it is no longer good for anything, except to be thrown out and trampled by men (Matt. 5:13). Let us scrutinize this meaning. Salt losing its saltiness necessitates its being "thrown out." *Strong's Concordance* instructs that losing "savor" in this passage means "to become insipid, dull, heedless, stupid." That brings to mind the sober quote from Revelation 3:16 about lukewarm Christians and God spitting (in the Greek, vomiting!) them out of His mouth. Is there a correlation between lukewarm Christendom and savorless salt?

Quick! Reach for the syringe and draw a blood sample to check the level of our saltiness and that of the Body of Christ. What would the lab report reveal? Medically, low sodium in the blood (severe hyponatremia) causes coma. As we inspect the status quo of the American Christian lifestyle, would it correlate with a blood level of little saltiness (i.e., low sodium)? Clinically are we near coma? If the Body of Christ, collectively, is comatose, then we cannot be leaders in chaos or disaster. We'd be too weak and unprepared.

Consider Isaiah's description of a soon-coming disaster and the need for leadership:

> A man will seize one of his brothers at his father's home, and say, "You have a cloak, you be our leader; take charge of this heap of ruins!" But in that day he will cry out, "I have no remedy. I have no food or clothing in my house; do not make me the leader of the people" (Isa. 3:6,7).

What an opportunity to be asked to lead in times of crisis! What a privilege to be able to lead, to provide light in darkness, peace in fear, order in confusion. However, unless we are properly trained and have pre-positioned supplies—spiritual as well as natural—our assistance will probably be minimal.

Arise, shine, for your light has come, and the glory of the Lord rises upon you. See, darkness covers the earth and thick darkness is over the peoples, but the Lord rises upon you and his glory appears over you. Nations will come to your light, and kings to the brightness of your dawn (Isa. 60:1-3).

Today, even in predisaster conditions, it seems that many Christians have lost or don't follow their spiritual compasses. Of course non-Christians have never had a compass by which to navigate through fierce storms, past dangerous reefs and into port. Jesus wants us to be so full of Him (the Light of the World) that we are a brilliant lighthouse beam, guiding bruised, battered survivors safely into Father's harbor.

How awesome to partner with God to bless others! We can make deliberate choices to do so. We can be ready with natural and spiritual skills. We can be salt and light! We can preserve physical and spiritual life! That is what this book is all about.

GOD'S TEARS . . . SALT RESIDUE

God beckons, "Ask of me, and I will make the nations your inheritance" (Ps. 2:8). Redeemed souls are the best inheritance we can take into eternity when we die. But we must ask God to give us His heart for souls if we are to obtain this inheritance. We need His heart to help others in desperation when it is not convenient or safe or cheap!

Are we ready for the kind of heart God has? The Scriptures reveal that Father God, Jehovah, has pain in His heart today, as we transition from one millennium to another. Centuries ago, speaking to Jeremiah, He said, "Speak this word to them: 'Let my eyes overflow with tears night and day without ceasing; for my virgin daughter—my people—have suffered a grievous wound, a crushing blow'" (Jer. 14:17). God is telling Jeremiah to tell the people that

He is crying! God is crying! His eyes are overflowing with tears from a broken heart for broken and lost humanity. That truth knocks the wind out of me! It makes my spirit groan in anguish.

How can we get God's cry in our hearts? Paul had this imparted to him. It's obvious from Romans 9:2, "I have great sorrow and unceasing anguish in my heart"; and Galatians 4:19, "My dear children, for whom I am again in the pains of childbirth until Christ is formed in you." Divine pain throbs in these passages.

To even hear that cry, we must allow God to circumcise our hearts, cutting away the cares and concerns of this world, the deceitfulness of riches, the desires for more and more *things*— even the preoccupation with our personal well-being. Being consumed by such things, we are forced to ignore the needs of millions who suffer without knowing how God's heart-cry moved Him to send Jesus to relieve their suffering! What can we give up in our lives—of our time, activities, effort, energy and finances—to intensify our saltiness?

In the last year, how many "frozen hearts" have been de-iced for God, by your witness?

It seems that once most Christians get their own eternity settled, once they personally name Jesus Christ as Savior, they forget about hell's reality because that horror has been resolved for them personally. If we believers in the United States had a visceral (gut) revelation of hell, I believe we would collectively be more aggressive for souls, more passionate, more committed and more steadfast about rescuing people from going to a for-ever-burning fire. The Bible exhorts:

> Rescue those being led away to death; hold back those staggering toward slaughter. If you say, "But we knew nothing about this," does not he who weighs the heart

perceive it? Does not he who guards your life know it? Will he not repay each person according to what he has done? (Prov. 24:11,12).

Scripture also says that if we as righteous persons do not warn the righteous who fall into evil, then their blood is on our hands (Ezek. 3:20). That is pretty sobering, isn't it? We often hear about the fluff, whipped cream and sugar of the blessings from following Jesus, but we do not frequently hear about our responsibilities based upon the critical nature of hell's eternal suffering. Isn't that really the greatest of all disasters? When we are born again, why are we left here on the earth? Isn't it spiritual malpractice if we don't completely and competently fulfill God's purpose?

CAN YOU FEEL HIS PAIN?

Theologians may argue that the pain in God's heart described in Jeremiah 14:17 was before the work of the Cross, and that it is thus now voided; or that God is described as suffering only for His "virgin daughter," Israel. However, having walked the soil of 41 nations, we have personally experienced the "fires of earthly hells" and God's unquenchable pain for tormented, oppressed, sick and destitute millions.

Walking the streets of Calcutta, Bangladesh and Pakistan has convinced us that God feels pain in heaven *today*. He looks down upon poverty and hunger, the hopelessness and disease, sin and bondage in those countries. Then He looks down on our country, sees how He has blessed her and how at times she has squandered the blessing. How can all this not break His heart?

"God so loved the world that he gave his one and only Son" (John 3:16). We know that verse so well that it appears to have lost its impact: the price of the sacrifice of a child. Think of sacrificing your child, my child, her child, so the world will not perish in hell! God does not want anyone to perish, but wants everyone to come to repentance (see 2 Pet. 3:9).

How many are perishing today, even in America? Millions? Will that increase as calamitous events deluge us? Hebrews 12:15 admonishes, "See to it that no one misses the grace of God." How many are missing the grace of God today in our country? It grieves the heart of God. Can't you feel the pain in the heart of Jesus? He wants to be the redemption of suffering people, but they are blinded and do not believe they need a Messiah. Listen to the agony in Jesus' heart as He cries, "O Jerusalem ... how often I have longed to gather your children together, as a hen gathers her chicks under her wings, but you were not willing" (Matt. 23:37).

Can the Body of Christ feel the anguish in the heart of God? Paul fervently expressed it: "I have great sorrow and unceasing anguish in my heart. For I could wish that I myself were cursed and cut off from Christ for the sake of my brothers, those of my own race, the people of Israel" (Rom. 9:2-4). Who of us would say, "Lord, cut me out of the Book of Life for the sake of my countrymen"?

Moses felt this distress in Exodus 32:32. When God's anger burned at disobedient Israel, Moses said in effect, "Take me out of Your book, and in exchange save the nation of Israel." Paul and Moses were humans just as we are; yet they were so impassioned with God's heart for people that they were each willing to spend forever away from Him in order that a whole nation could be saved. *That* is phenomenal disaster relief!

THE SUPREME DISASTER!

Could it be that Moses and Paul really believed that the *universe's greatest disaster is a soul experiencing the tragedy of the second death?* Would they have us focus on saving others from an eternity separated from God, light, peace, hope—eternally wretched and afflicted in the lake of fire and brimstone? Suddenly, discussions of inconvenient Y2K disruptions, the trauma of mass national disaster, even economic collapse, all pale against the backdrop of the second death. This revelation is our plumb line as we discuss other "lesser disasters" and our appropriate responses to them.

As I have heard John Osteen say, "Heaven is too real; hell is too hot; eternity is too long and time too short for us to play church in this hour!" How can we attempt to quantify the greatest disaster, the second death? First, insight emerges and grips us after a review of Scripture's description of hell. Second and conversely, as we inspect the precious price of redemption—Jesus' pain and passion in Gethsemane and on Calvary—God's heart-cry becomes an embedded chip in our perspective. *Being fully persuaded of these truths is the bedrock of crisis evangelism.*

Hell is a real place! It is . . .

The unquenchable fire, where their worm does not die, and the fire is not quenched (Mark 9:43,44, *NASB*).

Then death and Hades were thrown into the lake of fire. The lake of fire is the second death (Rev. 20:14). [The lost] will be tormented day and night for ever and ever (20:10).

But the cowardly, the unbelieving, the vile, the murderers, the sexually immoral, those who practice magic arts, the idolaters and all liars—their place will be in the fiery lake of burning sulfur. This is the second death (Rev. 21:8).

In hell, where he [the rich man] was in torment, he looked up and saw Abraham far away, with Lazarus by his side. So he called to him, "Father Abraham, have pity on me and send Lazarus to dip the tip of his finger in water and cool my tongue, because I am in agony in this fire" (Luke 16:23,24).

The Son of Man will send out his angels, and they will weed out of his kingdom everything that causes sin and all who do evil. They will throw them into the fiery furnace, where there will be weeping and gnashing of teeth (Matt. 13:41,42).

Then he will say to those on his left, "Depart from me, you who are cursed, into the eternal fire prepared for the devil and his angels" (Matt. 25:41).

Frequently, it appears, understanding the horrific realities of hell is like a sticky note stuck on our foreheads—only surface knowledge—instead of forceful truth brought to us by the Holy Spirit Himself. On a scale of 1 to 10, with 1 as lowest, what is the urgency level in the Body of Christ in America regarding the realities of hell and the millions headed there?

Natural disasters are increasing in frequency, complexity and expense. More people seem to be staggering toward slaughter at an alarming rate. We need rescue squads! When we get a revelation of a tormenting, miserable, hopeless, burning, eternal hell, then we are closer to the passion of God's heart.

FROM APATHY TO URGENCY

A great saboteur to this perspective is apathy. We are surgeons. Our specialties are often hallmarked by emergencies. Dr. Mark is a general surgeon. In trauma surgery for a gunshot wound to the chest with a ruptured aorta, Dr. Mark faces urgency! If he does not respond to critical situations with appropriate behavior, the patient suffers or dies.

As an obstetrician/gynecologist, I know that an OB specialist isn't usually required when a mother-to-be is laboring normally. But when complications create a crisis, I have to act very quickly or the baby might be compromised for the rest of his or her life. If I am in the nurses' lounge at a birthday party, having coffee and laughing, when my patient's baby's heart tones drop to 50, and I don't respond with immediate action, I am negligent and irresponsible. I can be held accountable for millions of dollars' worth of damage because I was not in place performing appropriate rescue procedures.

Amid the increasing crises and catastrophes of our world, will we find the Church "on coffee break" or "in the lounge"? Is the Body of Christ guilty of spiritual malpractice? Will we be soundly prepared and trained to respond? Are you ready to answer the forthcoming spiritual and literal 911 calls from distraught Americans facing impending calamities? We must be ready to dispatch EMS (Emergency *Ministry* Services) according to Jude 23: "Snatch others from the fire and save them; to others show mercy, mixed with fear—hating even the clothing stained by corrupted flesh."

Snatch people from the fire. Is that a blasé phrase? Just saunter over, sort of pick them up and get them out of the fire? No! It requires members of a fully equipped, competent, alert, risk-taking rescue squad who know the urgency of the situation!

JOIN GOD'S SEARCH AND RESCUE TEAM

To our astonishment, our loving Father instigated the universe's grandest search and rescue effort when He deployed His only Son. What an amazing mission—unparalleled in cost, history's most extravagant rescue, to negate the greatest calamity ever—

His creation careening toward the lake of fire (the second death) because of sin and rebellion.

> For the wages of sin is death, but the gift of God is eternal life in Christ Jesus our Lord (Rom. 6:23).

> For just as through the disobedience of the one man the many were made sinners, so also through the obedience of the one man the many will be made righteous (Rom. 5:19).

> We were therefore buried with him through baptism into death in order that, just as Christ was raised from the dead through the glory of the Father, we too may live a new life (Rom. 6:4).

Come and join me in a front-row seat at *the* great *Passion Play*. Can you hear with your heart as the Son prays, "Father, if it is possible, may this cup be taken from me. Yet not as I will, but as you will" (Matt. 26:39)? Are you ready to make this *your* prayer if God's discipline for believers and judgment for nonbelievers is loosed on the United States in order to crumble idols of materialism, self-centeredness and self-sufficiency? Is it God's will for us to pray that difficult times won't come, if millions would come to know the Savior only from acute need created by hardship, and thus miss hell? Is it selfish for us to beg God not to send difficulties? We pray, "In judgment, remember mercy." Is God's greatest mercy manifested in His judging our national condition?

Now notice as an angel enters from stage left to strengthen the Son of God. Listen carefully for the anguish and passion in Jesus' voice. And look! See the phenomenon of "hema ohydrosis"—blood oozing out of sweat glands. He is so stressed that the capillaries have ruptured into His sweat ducts! What an exorbitantly expensive hemorrhage to redeem our disastrous fate—eternity in hell!

Why such lavish abandonment to rescue the human race? Because God so loved the world:

> It was the Lord's will to crush him and cause him to suffer, and though the Lord makes his life a guilt offering, he will see his offspring and prolong his days, and the will of the Lord will prosper in his hand. After the suffering of his soul, he will see the light of life and be satisfied; by his knowledge my righteous servant will justify many, and he will bear their iniquities (Isa. 53:10,11).

Jesus did not just talk about coming to seek and save the lost. He left the comforts of heaven, putting His love into action to retrieve those headed for supreme disaster, the second death. His followers are not exempt from following in His footsteps:

> This is how we know what love is: Jesus Christ laid down his life for us. And we ought to lay down our lives for our brothers. If anyone has material possessions and sees his brother in need but has no pity on him, how can the love of God be in him? (1 John 3:16,17).

> Then he said to them all: "If anyone would come after me, he must deny himself and take up his cross daily and follow me. For whoever wants to save his life will lose it, but whoever loses his life for me will save it. What good is it for a man to gain the whole world, and yet lose or forfeit his very self? If anyone is ashamed of me and my words, the Son of Man will be ashamed of him when he

comes in his glory and in the glory of the Father and of the holy angels" (Luke 9:23-26).

For Christ's love compels us, because we are convinced that one died for all, and therefore all died. And he died for all, that those who live should no longer live for themselves but for him who died for them . . . . All this is from God, who reconciled us to himself through Christ and gave us the ministry of reconciliation (2 Cor. 5:14-18).

In the Greek, the word for *compel* means "lead away." Maybe more believers need a "compulsive disorder"—feeling compelled to leave self-preservation, comfort and security in favor of positioning their skills and finances to rescue suffering, dying people.

In 2 Corinthians 12:15 Paul said, "I will very gladly spend for you everything I have and expend myself as well ... [for the sake of the gospel]." *That is what God is asking every believer to do.* Whatever the difficulties, whatever crises may come, will it be said of us as it was said of Jesus that when He saw the crowds He was moved with compassion because they were harassed and helpless, like sheep without a shepherd (see Matt. 9:36)?

We in the United States have been insulated from many of the hardships, challenges and risks that face believers in Nepal, China, Pakistan, India and much of the Church in North Africa and Asia. Those regions are so foreign to us; calamities happen "way over there." Are we strong enough to adjust to the "culture shock" if conditions we formerly thought applied only "over there" (no electricity, sparse food, violent, desperate attempts for survival) are manifested here? Can we smoothly adapt? What if there is a prolonged crisis, not just a disruption? Or what if there are multiple smaller crisis scenarios superimposed one upon another? Our Sunday morning theology might abruptly take on new meaning. How would it be lived out? Philippians 2:21 is very, very sad: "Everyone looks out for his own interests, not those of Jesus Christ."

TOWARD A HEART TRANSPLANT

Every DNA molecule in us throbs as we pray for you, dear reader, that you will have great grace to consistently press into the heart of God, continually allowing yourself to be infused with His sovereign power and nature.

Oh, if we would only allow God Almighty to put His passion inside of us, we would be unstoppable. We would be on fire, radical, determined, demonstrating His power, anointing, presence, character. His nature would fill us so that we would have to burst it forth in service to others, or rupture our very selves! We would be like Jeremiah: "In my heart it [God's Word] becomes like burning fire shut up in my bones; and I am weary of holding it in. And I cannot endure it" (Jer. 20:9, *NASB*).

This is how God showed his love among us: He sent his one and only Son into the world that we might live through him. . . . Love is made complete among us so that we will have confidence on the day of judgment, because *in this world we are like him* (1 John 4:9,17, author's emphasis).

There is no fear in love. But perfect love drives out fear, because fear has to do with punishment. The one who fears is not made perfect in love (1 John 4:18).

Precious reader, we are not fearful. We are excited as we see God's hand in end-time events. Crisis conditions will accelerate and exaggerate opportunities to live out Jesus' example. Many may for the first time have a keen sense of the need to live for others in Jesus' name.

Jesus chose to be brutally killed to bring depraved humans to Himself. Are we so intent on following Him that we can make this deliberate, calculated, costly choice, too?

In our current time line, yet peering into eternity, let our prayer be, "Lord, make every breath I breathe and every molecule of energy I expend count eternally for the souls of others. Help me maximize every skill with which You have blessed me. O God, apprehend me! I surrender afresh as your love slave!"

BECOMING SALT AND LIGHT: HOW WE GOT STARTED

MARK NEUENSCHWANDER, M.D.

The woman seemed isolated and desperate as she took her place at the end of a long line at our clinic, a whitewashed shelter without electricity in a rural village in Bangladesh. Sheepishly, the woman came up to my wife, Dr. Betsy.

Through an interpreter, she related how she had been married to a Muslim man, but because of her inability to conceive she had been ostracized and her husband had thrown her out of her home. Her native family would no longer receive her, so she was reduced to being a prostitute in the village to survive.

Such sorrow on that face! As the story was related through the stoic male translator, Dr. Betsy began to weep aloud. Suddenly the universal language of tears crossed all barriers and the woman herself began to wail loud sobs and moans. As Dr. Betsy embraced her, tears streaming from their eyes, even our male translator was touched and could not hold back his emotions.

For me, the scene recalled Matthew's description of Jesus: "When he saw the crowds, he had compassion on them, because they were harassed and helpless, like sheep without a shepherd" (Matt. 9:36). At times like these the scalpel of the Holy Spirit would slice into our beings, revealing to us that we must demonstrate the love of Christ, not just speak about it. In times of crisis people need more than physical healing.

Dr. Betsy shared God's love with the woman, and told her that He had a wonderful plan for her life. We prayed that Jesus would be her husband, her lover and her friend. The Lord puts solitary persons into families (see Ps. 68:6), so we asked Him to place her into a family of people who would help to take care of her.

BURNING OUR BRIDGES

How had we come to be in Bangladesh? In 1986, Dr. Betsy and I looked at our new medical school faculty contracts and chose not to sign them. Instead we sold our cars, auctioned our furniture, and tried to sell our home. With hearts full of simple faith and a passionate desire to serve our Lord as career medical missionaries, we had very little concept of just how to begin. We simply stepped into the reality of the good works that the Lord had prepared in advance for us to do, even before the foundation of the world (see Eph. 2:10). As yet the path before us wasn't clear. We only knew that God's gifts and callings are without repentance, and that we were to obey the Great Commission of Jesus literally:

> Then Jesus came to them and said, "All authority in heaven and on earth has been given to me. Therefore, go and make disciples of all nations, baptizing them in the name of the Father and of the Son and of the Holy Spirit, and teaching them to obey everything I have commanded you. And surely I am with you always, to the very end of the age" (Matt. 28:18-20).

"Go into all the world and preach the good news to all creation. Whoever believes and is baptized will be saved, but whoever does not believe will be condemned. And these signs will accompany those who believe: In my name they will drive out demons; they will speak in new tongues; they will pick up snakes with their hands; and when they drink deadly poison, it will not hurt them at all; they will place their hands on sick people, and they will get well." . . . Then the disciples went out and preached everywhere, and the Lord worked with them and confirmed his word by the signs that accompanied it (Mark 16:15-20).

The supernatural knowing that our destiny would be to fulfill the Great Commission was revealed in our spirits shortly after we each had born-again experiences. We knew God's word to Jeremiah was applicable to us: "Before I formed you in the womb I knew you, and before you were born I consecrated you; I have appointed you a prophet to the nations" (Jer. 1:5, *NASB*).

Betsy had a wonderful born-again experience while working at Ridge Crest Southern Baptist Camp one summer between two college years. She enthusiastically began witnessing in her sphere of influence. Later, at medical university, she had the privilege of bringing fellow medical students to the Savior, and even Jews to the Messiah. It was her psychiatric rotation in her senior year that catapulted her into a study of Jesus and demons in the Gospels. After maturing in this area, she began ministering deliverance as an intern.

As for me, I had attended parochial schools and even a Jesuit college, but did not surrender to the lordship of Jesus Christ until I was in medical school. This awesome, life-changing experience occurred only after a personal tragedy that left me emotionally devastated. The Lord used this to shake the false, egocentric foundations of my life.

Initially, my desire was to drop out of medical school and attend Bible school. However, after godly counsel from Betsy and the seasoned medical missionaries Dr. Ralph Bethea and wife, Lizette, I realized that perhaps God would be more honored if I finished my medical school training. The compulsion to bring others into the Kingdom led me to make it a priority to personally witness to at least half of my 100 medical school classmates in various clinical rotations within 12 months. Later, I will recount how I paid a price in my residency for being salt and light in the operating room of a Memphis hospital.

While in clinical practice, we have prayed for many patients and have seen many of them divinely healed. Their recovery has often been confirmed by lab or X ray. We witnessed to our patients in United States practice settings as well as overseas. We are convinced that you do not have to go to foreign soil to see the book of Acts lived out.

LAUNCHING OUT TOGETHER

Before we met and while she was a senior medical student, Dr. Betsy worked with Arab refugees in the Gaza Strip of Israel. The following year I spent 10 weeks in Bangalore, India, at a mission hospital. Each of us had been willing to obey God's call on our lives, and were prepared to go to the mission field alone. Our loving Father, however, had a more tender and perfect plan. He supernaturally put Dr. Betsy and me together to work in His harvest. In the beginning, we could not possibly foresee that we would be going to many different nations together, yet we have now had the privilege of serving the King of kings in more than

40 countries! For the last several years my nickname for Dr. Betsy has been "Mother of Nations."

The description of Daniel, Shadrach, Meshach and Abednego in Daniel 1:3-7 became pivotal verses for us during our early training years. I believed that the Lord wanted us to become like these young Hebrew men in medicine—"skilful in all wisdom, and cunning in knowledge, and understanding science" (v. 4, *KJV*). We embarked on additional training, not realizing that this would require each of us to complete two residencies apiece. After four years of medical school, this required nine years of arduous internship training and residency for me (general surgery and family practice) and seven years for Dr. Betsy (obstetrics and gynecology, surgery and family practice). During all this time we had tried to the best of our ability to feed our spirits despite the long hours. The Lord used the preceding verses describing Daniel's training to become Spirit and Life to us.

After we completed our residencies and served for 18 months on a medical school faculty, we sensed that it was time for us to launch out into the deep. We decided to study with Youth With A Mission's Crossroads Discipleship Training School for three months. After completing our time in the classroom with YWAM, we spent some time in Thailand before being confronted with the disturbing question of whether we were willing to work in the garbage dump of Calcutta.

Compelled to answer yes, we first worked with Mark Buntain's Mission of Mercy Hospital in Calcutta, India, in close proximity to Mother Teresa's home for the dying. The pervasive, pungent smell of the city, the millions of flies and large black crows that swarmed over the garbage heaps carrying sickness and death graphically brought home to us the need for the prevention of diseases, not just the cure. As we treated hundreds of patients with scabies skin infections, we quickly realized the need for clean and sanitary living conditions.

Like sweeping the sand on a seashore, we immediately grasped that healing the overwhelming physical needs of this great populace was a human impossibility. If only we could duplicate and multiply ourselves by ten, one hundred or a thousandfold!

THE NEED FOR SUPERNATURAL POWER

We also keenly sensed our human frailty as we witnessed the tremendous need for the supernatural power of God to be demonstrated. Muslims and Hindus needed the evidence of miracles that would demand a verdict. So we augmented our medical clinics with preaching and teaching meetings and other opportunities to lay hands upon sick people and pray for them in Calcutta and other regions of India.

Once, in a remote village in southern India, we were asked to visit an elderly man lying on a sickbed. Hardly a ray of light could find its way through the doorway of his dismal dwelling, for it seemed that the whole village had crowded into the small opening. At first glance into the man's hollow, sunken eyes, we sensed the presence of demonic power in his body. Calling the name of Jesus under the anointing of the Holy Spirit, we commanded the evil spirits to leave! A power struggle ensued as Satan fought for his prey. The back of the man's body curled and contorted backward in an inhuman form, and he writhed like a snake. But the demons were no match for the sinless Son of God! The man was set free—hallelujah!

Soon the news of the power of the name of Jesus swept through that village, and many accepted the lordship of Jesus. My good friend Sam Taylor, an Anglo-Indian, has helped train thousands of people to establish churches in southeast Asia through similar power encounters at his Bible training center in Rayakota.

Such incidents resulted in our being advertised, without our knowledge, as "healing evangelists" as we made plans to work in another city. Consequently, we were unable to conduct a medical clinic, so we just preached the gospel. We were literally amazed when we watched Jesus confirm His preached word by supernaturally healing people. He even healed two Muslim hecklers who cut the power to the light sources on the perimeter of the crusade ground.

At the end of one of these meetings a young Hindu man, who had been discharged from a nearby hospital with end-stage lymphoma, came to us. His neck was grossly enlarged and felt hard as wood. He could afford neither radiation nor chemotherapy. After hearing in the crusade meeting that nothing was too difficult for Jesus and that He still heals today, he asked for prayer. God immediately gave a gift of faith to Dr. Betsy, and she heard these words pouring from her mouth: "When Jesus Christ heals you, will you renounce all of your Hindu idols and live for Jesus Christ alone?"

She then prayed a long prayer with her eyes closed, hoping that God would supernaturally heal the man then and there. When she opened her eyes, she was disappointed to see that the lumps and masses in his neck were still visible. However, two months later we received a letter from the Indian pastor who helped conduct the crusade, saying that within a short time after we had prayed for the man, the masses completely disappeared! He also renounced his Hindu idols and was actively serving in the Lord's Church! Praise God!

MULTITUDES IN THE VALLEY OF DECISION

Later we worked in Bangladesh, a predominantly Muslim country where the ostracized woman whom we mentioned earlier lived.

We assisted in surgery at a relatively new Christian hospital 14 hours away from the capital. Travel to this rural setting was quite a feat! It began with an interesting ride on a primitive train, continued with handcarrying our luggage for several hundred yards across railroad ties to catch a ferry across an unstable river, hopping onto a human rickshaw, and finally climbing aboard an oxcart to complete our journey!

For many hours we traveled past what appeared to be millions of people who had never heard nor would ever hear a viable gospel witness! We grappled with the words of Joel 3:14: "Multitudes, multitudes in the valley of decision! For the day of the Lord is near in the valley of decision." We saw desperate needs and unimaginable diseases while working as surgeons and clinicians. We despaired that the task was so enormous and that there were only two of us. The words of Jesus rang in our spiritual ears: "The harvest is plentiful but the workers are few. Ask the Lord of the harvest, therefore, to send out workers into his harvest field" (Matt. 9:37,38).

Some parts of North India are staunchly Hindu, while others are predominantly Muslim. It was in this setting that we witnessed man's inhumanity to man. It cruelly illustrated that the words of Jesus are so true, when He said, "The love of money is the root of all evil" (1 Tim. 6:10). We had just gone to bed in a hospital compound when suddenly we heard loud screams. Several people were bringing a patient in on a rolling cart. The patient was so badly charred that at first I could not discern if the thin body was a man or a woman. After obtaining a history from neighbors, we learned that this was a woman whose family had not completely paid the dowry for her arranged marriage to her husband. In retaliation they doused her and the four meters of cloth in the *sari* she wore in kerosene and set her ablaze like a human torch.

Although the practice is outlawed by the Indian constitution, it was all too real for this woman. As we examined her, we were horrified by her agonizing, gasping breathing, and the pus around her eye sockets. She died within a few hours.

Although we had seen many tragedies while training in charity governmental hospitals in the United States, we felt nauseated, and our knees almost buckled at this sight. We were faced with the sobering reality of a soul slipping into an eternity of hell with the appalling smell of burning hair and flesh being exchanged for that of burning sulfur and an unquenchable fire! Not only did this woman experience a living hell on earth, but now she would experience an eternal hell. The words of Paul the apostle became very real:

> For there is no difference between Jew and Gentile—the same Lord is Lord of all and richly blesses all who call on him, for, "Everyone who calls on the name of the Lord will be saved." How, then, can they call on the one they have not believed in? And how can they believe in the one of whom they have not heard? And how can they hear without someone preaching to them? And how can they preach unless they are sent? As it is written, "How beautiful are the feet of those who bring good news!" (Rom. 10:12-15).

Further, the words of Jesus echoed in our souls: "I am the way, and the truth, and the life; no one comes to the Father, but through Me (John 14:6, *NASB*).

In the midst of the busy Howrah train station in Calcutta, which accommodates 2 million people daily, we had to step over dead bodies covered with maggots. The tragic drama of the souls that had departed these bodies to most likely spend an eternity in a lake of fire and brimstone did not escape our spirits. The reality of souls experiencing the greatest disaster of all, where the fire is not quenched and the worm does not die, caused us to cry even more urgently to the Lord to send effective laborers and multiplication strategies to train those who had the ability to effect change.

Thankfully, lest we would despair at the suffering around us, there were other times when we experienced the joy of the Lord. For Dr. Betsy and me, there is no greater ecstasy than seeing people respond affirmatively to the life-saving message we proclaim. We have had the high privilege of seeing many precious souls born into the kingdom of heaven.

TRAINING OTHERS FOR MULTIPLICATION

We returned to the United States in 1988 for a time of rest and refreshing, seeking the Lord, and for additional Bible and mission training. While here, in answer to our increasingly fervent prayers for multiplication strategies, God conceived and birthed through Dr. Betsy and me what was to become a training seminar called the Spiritual Skills Course for Professionals.

Because professionals are ordinarily trained to be analytical, skeptical, and objective, this seminar was designed to build faith in those attending. We did this by utilizing credible, professional teachers the audience could respect. The speakers related their personal experiences and miracles they have individually seen, even how God raised people from the dead through their hands! It was to be a time of intense study and prayer for the unreached countries of our world, asking the Holy Spirit for strategies to reach each diverse country. Designed to be a time of practical impartation and ministry, our slogans became what we had learned as medical interns, such as "See one, do one and teach one." You can read about something all day but without hands-on experience you will not remember it or be able to practice it!

We sensed that the Lord wanted us to capture this first school on videotape. However, the projected cost was $75,000. We had only $3,000 in the bank, and the school was to begin in less than three months. We allowed discouragement and our rationalization to convince ourselves that it was not feasible. I told the Lord, "We cannot have this school because there is no time to advertise and no money to professionally videotape it. Besides, busy professionals have their schedules arranged several months in advance."

That night the Lord awoke me, and I spent some time weeping before Him, asking His forgiveness for grieving His Holy Spirit through my disobedience and lack of faith. As we launched out in faith, we were able to conduct the school with excellence for only $24,000. A lady we barely knew said the Lord told her to write us a check for $20,000 before the school began. A few days before it started, the rest of the money came in.

Although only 12 people attended that first school, the investment in time and money has paid fabulous dividends. Many of those 12 have worked with us on different mission fields and several have become full-time missionaries themselves! And since then over 1,800 people from various walks of life have attended these seminars in different countries.

We have taken these videotapes into India, Malaysia, Eastern Europe and the former Soviet Union, primarily targeting professionals and "leaders of the soil." Periodically, we have also continued to conduct seminars for professionals within the United States, being privileged to train many people. Now we were multiplying!

HOLY SPIRIT STRATEGIES

Our ministry took on a new dimension before one of our Skills Courses in India when we were praying on a rooftop in Bangalore. The Holy Spirit gave a different word to me, and to each of the female intercessors on our team. To one was given the word *penetrate*, to another the word *infiltrate*, to another *multiply* and to me the word *establish*. Although we did not comprehend what this meant at the time, when we returned to the United States, the Lord made clear that He wanted us to believe Him for strategies of Penetration, Infiltration, and Multiplication to Establish His healing, delivering and saving presence. We came to realize that He was actually doing this through our work overseas.

As we assessed the rural health care needs of India, we asked for Holy Spirit strategies. We found that 80 percent of the diseases of India could be prevented by knowing and practicing simple techniques of nutrition, sanitation and hygiene. We learned that, in general, Hindus and Muslims lack the intrinsic motivation from the love of God to position themselves to help hurting, distressed people. Therefore, in three different places, we spent two weeks teaching Bible school students who desired to work in the villages of rural India. We imparted to them practical skills that would give them favor with Muslims and Hindus. They became the equivalent of "barefoot doctors," but with the gospel message. The Lord especially blessed these endeavors in 1990.

At the same locations we also taught the power of praise and worship, and the principles of spiritual warfare and overcoming the forces of darkness. Some of the students we taught are still using these principles today as they go out into villages ministering to people who need physical healing, literacy, etc. God's *penetration* and *infiltration* are still at work! Hallelujah!

In January 1997, I attended and taught workshops at a conference for 10,000 students in Hyderabad, India. A young man
with the praise and worship team, Valson Abraham, approached
me and related that in 1990 we had spent extra time with him
teaching him about prayer and praise. He said the truths we had
imparted to him had extraordinarily impacted him and encouraged him to follow the Lord. Today he is the praise and worship
leader of the largest full gospel church in Hyderabad, a predominantly Muslim city of several million people. We rejoiced at this
marvelous display of God's strategy of *establishment!*

A VISION OF INDIA AND EUROPE

The Lord gave us a portrait of India in 1991. In it the country was
like a huge fruit plantation filled with gigantic trees. The trees
were so high that ladders were essential to obtain the precious
fruit. In contrast, the Lord revealed to us that the seasonal fruit
in Eastern Europe was so ripe that it was falling off the trees. The
wrong harvesters were gathering the plentiful fruit. They were
not Christians.

Struggling with the decision to leave our beloved India, the
Lord confirmed through a magazine article Dr. Betsy was reading
that we were to go into Eastern Europe. The article described the
spiritual hunger there, and also the desire of doctors in Romania
to be updated with Western medical knowledge and techniques
that had been denied them for decades.

A short time later we attended a Christian Scientific Seminar
in Romania. It did not take long to discover that the needs in
Eastern Europe were vastly different than those of India. In
1991, the disasters that were prevalent in Eastern Europe were
primarily political, social, medical and economic. Infrastruc-
tures were either tottering or had already collapsed. The grip of

the police state had been partially loosened, and people craved new ideas. When we fulfilled their craving for scientific knowledge, we found that they were very grateful and would attend spiritual seminars if taught by the same group of professionals.

Not long afterwards, we were in Sofia, the capital of Bulgaria. The Lord gave us favor with government officials, who allowed us to bring in pharmaceuticals duty-free. We brought a team of professionals from various backgrounds to meet the needs of professionals in the city of Bourgas, on the Black Sea. Hosted by our long-time missionary friends Larry and Kay Mills of Labor of Love, this multifaceted team consisted of an evangelist of Middle Eastern descent, a Swedish praise and worship group and our international team of professionals. A third team of health-care providers conducted medical clinics for the general populace. We taught scientific updates in medicine, nursing and engineering for two hours, and spiritual matters for six to eight hours for a week before the evangelistic crusade. About 75 people attended and all of them received the Lord!

God did many miracles in the medical clinics and during the crusade. These professionals, who had just been taught about the power of God, observed for the first time in their lives the scriptural evidence of signs and wonders that demanded a verdict. How can I describe to you the excitement of our graduates as they prayed for the sick to be healed in the name of Jesus and saw miracles happen before their very eyes! This glory was matched only by the people who received the healings.

After the crusade, it was one of the extraordinary privileges of my life to be one of 10 men who baptized 1,000 people in the frigid waters of the Black Sea. Our spirits and voices soared in exaltation to Almighty God as souls were *multiplied* to His kingdom!

TO RUSSIA WITH LOVE

The following year (1992), we utilized similar God-inspired strategies in the former Soviet Union. Effective seminars were held in St. Petersburg for professionals, including medical students from the prestigious Leningrad Medical University.

By the time we got to Moscow, our international team had grown to 22 members, and we were able to give scientific updates in business and economics, dentistry, nursing and engineering. Through prayer and intercession, the Lord provided 90 people for this seminar. Seventy of the attendees were staff or students from the renowned Kremlin Nursing School. Much hard work was required, but our team members felt privileged to baptize many of these students in the bathtubs of our hotel, men team members baptizing men, and women baptizing women.

Anticipation was intense when we headed for the Muslim part of the former Soviet Union. After spending six months praying for strategies of multiplication in this region, we were led by the Lord supernaturally, through Korean-American physician Dr. Chishoo Choi, to Pastor David Kim, the senior pastor of Grace Korean Church in Los Angeles. Eighty percent of the entire budget of this church goes into missions!

Pastor Kim had already started a seminary in Moscow. He introduced us to a quiet, gentle man of Korean descent, Kim Sam Seong. Raised as a Buddhist in South Korea, he had found the Lord during his training as a lawyer. After attending seminary in Germany, he accepted a mission assignment in Almaty, the capital of Kazakstan. Kim Sam Seong and his lovely wife, Sunko, had worked two to three years pioneering a 500-member multiethnic church. Their fervent prayers had been to reach the leaders of their city with the gospel and to have a church of 1,000 members by the end of the year. He warmly welcomed us and invited us to his beautiful city of 1.2 million people, not far from the border of China. They boasted one of the world's fastest iceskating rinks.

When we arrived in Almaty, our team had grown to over 40 people from six different nationalities. We were introduced to a government official who asked if we were with WHO (World Health Organization) or UNICEF. Answering in the negative, we explained that we were all professionals from various walks of life and from different countries, who were paying our own way and volunteering our time to meet and assist the people of his city. We were given free TV and press coverage over this second largest geographic republic of the former Soviet Union!

Disasters of epic proportions faced the city of Almaty. The country's five-year economic plan was in shambles. Medical school students had left classes to sell wares on the streets and become taxi drivers. Kazakstan was sitting on the second largest oil and natural gas reservoir known at that time, but the know-how and infrastructure to take it out of the ground was not available. There were no pharmaceutical factories to make even basic antibiotics or aspirin. Everyone wanted to know how to make money.

The Holy Spirit had spoken to Dr. Betsy ahead of time, and instructed us to have intense, one-week seminars for agnostic, Marxist and Muslim professionals in engineering, dentistry, nursing, medicine, business and computer instruction for government officials. Further, we were to purchase 10 laptop computers with Russian software and carry these in our backpacks.

In this opportune setting, 700 professionals attended one week of our scientific sessions at the International Cultural Center. A nominal tuition fee was used to help provide a lunch for them. Continued prayer was sent heavenward for a spiritual breakthrough. On the third day, during the tea breaks in the morning and afternoon, academic instructors on our team began to share why they had come. Over the next two to three days they shared the love of God and the reality of His son Jesus in their lives. These professionals had never experienced the love of God, and they tangibly felt this love expressed from our team members.

Downstairs a free medical clinic was being offered, featuring the *Jesus* film in their language. Medical personnel were also praying for their needs and the needs of the people. At week's end, on the last day, a Persian male physician, born in Iran but trained in Sweden and the United States, gave a powerful, loving gospel message at tea breaks. Over 90 percent of these leaders accepted Jesus Christ! I gently but strongly encouraged them to attend the next week of biblical instruction on how to become a better professional. Over 500 of them left their jobs to attend these sessions full-time the next week; and 110 of them, including many Muslim professionals, were willing to be water baptized. We did this in an enclosed, heated swimming pool—with snow on the ground outside.

The next week, an open-air healing crusade was held by a physician friend of ours. God once again confirmed His Word with many miracles, which were the first our students had seen. Professional videotapes of the seminars in Eastern Europe and the former Soviet Union were left in their hands for distribution and dissemination.

A strong effort was made to be sure everyone who attended clearly understood what the lordship of Jesus involves. We did not want them to have a counterfeit message of salvation without surrender and lordship. Further, the elementary doctrines of the Christian faith were carefully explained, a "foundation of repentance from acts that lead to death, and of faith in God, instruction about baptisms, the laying on of hands, the resurrection of the dead, and eternal judgment" (Heb. 6:1,2).

A wonderful example of this was a physician in a group practice with three Muslim colleagues. He quizzed a member of our team one day before the baptismal service. "What do I say to my colleagues and to my family?" he asked. "I may be isolated by my decision to follow this Jesus." Overwhelmed with joy, I watched him run up and be the last one to join the baptismal line. We will never forget the rapture of that scene! Beautiful music was playing in the background at the swimming pool, and we knew angels in heaven were watching and rejoicing with us as these priceless souls were ushered into the Kingdom! The Lord was showing us that one does not need to go to seminary to be a disciple or even a disciple maker! If those who attended these sessions put into practice what they had learned, they too would become disciple makers.

The week after we left Almaty there was a big national conference of many religious cult groups. Because they had plenty of money, they rented the indoor wrestling arena that we had tried to schedule for our crusade. Even though our crusade had to be held outside in the snow of December, we were not concerned about our 500 new leaders going astray. They had graduated from our two-week training sessions. They had handled the real "currency" long enough to be well able to distinguish the counterfeit!

In this potentially volatile society, where persecution from other groups was a strong possibility, Pastor Kim realized that cell groups were the way to expand and capture all this new fruit coming into the Kingdom. His strategy was similar to that of Pastor Kriengsak Joseph, the shepherd over Hope of Bangkok Church, the largest church in Thailand, who had to go underground for a short time because of government persecution. Pastor Kim was also flexible about how cell groups were to function. Compared with St. Petersburg and Moscow, we saw much more fruit and a longer-lasting impact in this region because we were working with a pastor who had a passion to reach the leaders of his society, had a vision for cell-group multiplication and maintained a godly example of a white-hot prayer life!

In 1997 I had the privilege of seeing and hearing Pastor David Kim at the Praying with Power Conference in Colorado Springs. Pastor Kim Sam Seong from Almaty, Kazakstan, was also a featured speaker. His church had grown to 1,000 members by the end of 1992, and now his church is several thousand members strong!

One of our spiritual skills instructors, Dr. Marty Bassett, an endocrinologist from Oregon, had moved with his family to Almaty. In the spring of 1996 Pastor Kim Sam Seong's church was featured in the Evangelical Missions Quarterly as one of the two model churches for Central Asia. Pastor Kim Sam Seong related to me that many of those who were in key leadership in his church received their foundation teaching in our seminars. I asked Marty to answer my question honestly: "What percentage of those we instructed were still in the church and replicating?" He said between one-third and one-half. Although we wished the percentage were higher, we were grateful that so many were being "salt and light" in their communities and professions.

REVISING AND EXPANDING OUR CURRICULUM

Our spiritual skills courses have now been renamed a more fitting title: Spiritual Skills/Warfare Institutes. In addition to the topics already mentioned, others include: Identificational Repentance; Breaking Generational Curses; Prayer That Dispossesses; How to

Hear God's Voice and Obey; The Cost of Discipleship; The Anointing of the Holy Spirit; God's Heart for the Unreached; Myths About Missions; Cell Group Multiplication Strategies in Diverse Settings; Country Study Presentations; Worship and Intercession; and Ministry Techniques for Children and Cell Groups.

We always spend much time praying for the people who attend these seminars because it will be a struggle for them to face the spiritual battles to come and to practice what they receive by impartation and instruction. Particularly for professionals, the battle is against the temptation of pride in their intellectual capacities and earning abilities. Many are in debt/spending cycles that must be broken. Jesus warned, concerning the seed of the Word going into the soil, that "the worries of this life, the deceitfulness of wealth and the desires for other things come in and choke the word, making it unfruitful" (Mark 4:19).

The spiritual rewards for following the Lord, making disciples and overcoming to the end are great. We feel extremely blessed that Father God has allowed us to work in His vineyard and to gather His harvest. Perhaps you, too, have had many similar experiences, or perhaps reading our experiences has awaked a desire within you to be more salty in the days ahead!

Signs of the Times and Your Destiny

Mark Neuenschwander, M.D.

Our world is filled with unnerving and disturbing events. It is so unpredictable. Or is it? Jesus Christ made the most famous prediction when He answered His followers' question, "What will be the sign of your coming and of the end of the age?" (Matt. 24:3). Although Jesus clearly states that no one except God the Father knows the actual day of His return, He did describe the last days:

> You will hear of wars and rumors of wars, but see to it that you are not alarmed. Such things must happen, but the end is still to come. Nation will rise against nation, and kingdom against kingdom. There will be famines and earthquakes in various places. All these things are the beginning of birth pains (Matt. 24:6-8).

Observing these signs, we must acknowledge that the words of Jesus are becoming true before our eyes. Furthermore, such signs are increasing. The question is no longer *whether* wars, rumors of wars, plagues, famines, pestilences and earthquakes in various places will occur. The question is *when* and *where* they will occur, what we are to do for our loved ones, and how we can best position ourselves to minister in the crises ahead.

Many are concerned by the economic fragility of the industrialized nations, the threat of chemical or biological warfare and terrorism, the increasing number of natural disasters, the repercussions of the computer millennium bug (Y2K), and even global warming with the melting of large Antarctic ice masses and the flooding of many coastal cities that could result.

If some of the predicted scenarios actually occur, there will be widespread disruptions in the infrastructure and the efficient running of our societies. But consider how the crisis level would be complicated and magnified if more than one of these disasters should occur at the same time.

We in the United States are now all too familiar with disaster. We reeled in disbelief and cried in anguish at the Oklahoma City Murrah Federal Building explosion. We shuddered in terror at the bombing of the World Trade Center. We acknowledged the destructive power of the ever-grinding tectonic plates with the devastation in the Los Angeles earthquake. Add some biological warfare or terrorism superimposed on top of any of those, and we have a real mess. Thousands of people could die, become maimed or lose their homes, while the emergency disaster relief systems, firefighters, police and medical personnel are paralyzed because of malfunctioning communications and equipment.

Worldwide, similar events could be added to the chronicle of tornadoes, hurricanes and floods that occur almost continually in some location or another. Let us focus on each threat in more depth.

WORLDWIDE ECONOMIC INSTABILITY

In 1998, the U.S. stock market fell 20 percent from July to October. Many young brokers had never seen such wild gyrations of the market. A September issue of *U.S. News and World Report* stated that 19 of Japan's largest banks are almost insolvent and in need of a government bailout. With trillions of dollars of bad loans, the Japanese problem is much larger than the U.S. Savings & Loan bailout several years ago.

In mid-September of 1998 the Russian *ruble* lost more than two-thirds of its former value. While we were working and traveling in the Pacific Rim in 1997, the Malaysian *ringat* and the South Korean *won* dropped to less than half their values with stomach-wrenching speed.

The United States is not immune to these problems; nor will Christians escape economic hardship just because we follow Christ. Christians in South Korea have traditionally gathered for 5:30 A.M. prayers since 1910. Despite this practice throughout Seoul, we personally know dedicated, competent Christian professionals there (some doctors and nurses who worked with us teaching seminars in India) who were unable to find employment when their hospital closed in the spring of 1997.

Indonesia, the fourth largest nation, was an extremely prosperous country with rich oil reserves and sufficient rice to feed its large populace. Some of the wealthiest people in the world reside there. Only a few years ago, many large high-rise buildings were being constructed in the capital, Jakarta, and luxury automobiles crowded the streets. But in May 1998, sudden financial collapse caused an 80 percent drop in the value of its currency, and there was widespread famine.

There were severe riots throughout the country. Dr. Joseph Paul Ozawa, Harvard graduate and senior clinical psychologist for the Ministry of Community Development in Singapore, and Dr. Larry Gee, a U.S. family physician (both faculty members in our Disaster Response Schools), responded to the crisis. They reported that at least 1,200 people were killed and there was mass destruction of businesses. More than 130 ethnic Chinese women were raped, some by gangs, before they were murdered.

Prior to these events, cruel persecution of Christians broke out. From 1995–1997, in this, the world's largest Muslim nation, 131 churches were burned to the ground. The government was almost toppled and President Suharto was forced to step down. As of October 1998, an estimated 40 to 80 million people in Indonesia (a population the size of New York, California and Texas combined) were on the verge of starvation.

NUCLEAR, CHEMICAL/BIOLOGICAL, COMPUTER AND ECO-TERRORISM

Nuclear. An April 1997 *Reader's Digest* article describes hundreds of poorly protected nuclear storage sites in Russia, where much of the nuclear material is almost unguarded. There are over 1,000 tons of weapons-grade highly enriched uranium and plutonium available in the former Soviet Union to anyone with the money to buy it. It would take only three pounds of this material to destroy a city. *Readers's Digest* points out that anyone can buy plans for nuclear bombs over the Internet, and most of the needed electronics are available through large electronic mail-order houses.

Chemical agents. At the time of the tragic bombing of the Oklahoma City Murrah Federal Building in April 1995, we had just arrived at the First International Congress on Disaster Response in Shanghai, China. We were leading a 32-member team from four nations, and giving six papers to the Chinese delegates. The president of the World Association of Emergency Medicine expressed his condolences to our team, and sent a fax to the governor of Oklahoma. We were shocked. Here we were trying to help another country and our own homeland was under attack!

The sarin gas attack in a Tokyo subway the same year—the first major chemical or biological gas attack in an industrialized society in recent times—caught the world's attention. Unsuspecting Japanese businessmen and women had initial symptoms of runny nose and chest tightening, progressing to muscle weakness and tremors. Later, some died from muscular paralysis and suffocation.

Sarin was first available at the end of World War II. Allied forces also seized large quantities of tabun, the first chemical nerve agent, invented as a pesticide by a German chemist in 1934. Discoveries of such materials that had implications for warfare had to be reported to the German government. By the end of the war, German scientists had synthesized 2,000 new organo-phosphorous compounds, including sarin. In the mid-1950s a group of more stable agents with more than 10 times the poisonous toxicity of sarin was synthesized.

Now, according to the CIA, the country of Iran alone can produce 1,000 tons of chemical agents every year. It is believed that Iran has stockpiles of these chemical nerve and blister agents (i.e., mustard gas) as well as cyanide and phosgene.

Biological agents. When released in relatively large quantities, the chemical agent sarin can affect hundreds to thousands of people. But an equivalent amount of botulinus toxin, the most powerful biological agent, which can be released by aerosol using a cheap agricultural spray device, could kill 10 to 15 million people! Such biological agents have therefore been called "a poor man's atomic bomb."

Biological agents can be easily hidden and are hard to detect. Released from an aircraft with proper weather and wind conditions, they can spread over 20 to 30 miles. The deadly bacteria anthrax produces a spore that survives in soil and water for years and is difficult to eradicate. We live in a sinister age.

Computer hackers. "Stay home, have a beer, sabotage the U.S. government" was the title of an article in *U.S. News and World Report* in its July 13, 1998 report on computer hackers. Such electronic terrorism against new and unsuspecting targets is increasing in America.

According to CIA director George Tenet, it is possible for a computer hacker employed by a foreign government to attack another country's information and computer systems. In February 1998, the FBI raided the homes of two California high school sophomores who had assaulted the Pentagon, NASA and a nuclear weapons research lab. It was described by the deputy defense secretary as "the most organized and systematic attack" on U.S. computers ever discovered.

Eco-Terrorism. Upset that an adjacent tract of land would be used for leisure and business purposes threatening the extinction of the lynx, eco-terrorists claimed responsibility for simultaneous fires that burned several buildings at the famous Vail Ski Resort in October 1998. (The U.S. Forest Service stated that the lynx had not been sighted on this land for over 25 years.)

Increasingly, people are taking radical ideas of justice into their own hands. These are days like those in Israel as noted in the last verse of the book of Judges: "In those days there was no king in Israel; everyone did what was right in his own eyes" (*NASB*). However, the Bible also states that "There is a way which seems right to a man, but its end is the way of death" (Prov. 14:12, *NASB*).

WARS INVOLVING DISPLACED PEOPLES

In June 1995, a small delegation from our International Health

Services foundation attended a debriefing of firefighters and medical personnel in Oklahoma City. Among other experts we heard Jeff Lillibridge, M.D., Ph.D, from the Communicable Disease Center in Atlanta and the Office of Disaster Management in Washington, D.C., who has extensive international experience. He said, "At this time there are an estimated 30 to 40 million people who are displaced or seeking asylum in other nations. This number increases by 10,000 daily. There is a new refugee camp or settlement happening every week."

In 1995, Michael Little, president of Christian Broadcasting Network, told a group of Christian leaders that there were currently 38 ethnic conflicts occurring in the world. In 1997 the United Nations Commissioner on Refugees said refugees from such wars had increased to an estimated 50 million people.

PLAGUES AND PESTILENCES

Another sign of the last days will be increases in plagues and pestilences. But as far back as the 14th century, the bubonic plague or "Black Death" almost decimated London and ravaged Europe. An estimated 25 percent of the population died from 1347 through 1352. Caused by a bacteria that lives in rats and other rodents, the disease was transmitted to human beings by fleas from infected rats. It was then transmitted from human to human by inhaled droplets. A few years ago, the government of India was alarmed when the plague occurred in milder form near Bombay.

Although we have antibiotics today, they are not always available when needed the most. Also, they are not effective against viruses, flu epidemics and increasingly resistant bacteria. With large numbers of displaced peoples living in close quarters without the ability to dispose of sewage properly, there is always potential risk of epidemics of disastrous proportions. Recently, the scourge of AIDS and the lethal Ebola virus has exposed the lurking dangers in the world of viruses.

In 1994, war between the Tutsi and Hutu tribes in Rwanda caused 300,000 refugees to flee Rwanda and Burundi into Goma, Zaire. At times 10,000 people an hour were crossing their respective borders. Many dead bodies were thrown into Lake Victoria, contaminating the water supply for the surrounding countries. Over 30 of our medical and nursing graduates assisted in the relief effort with Operation Blessing, and reported multitudes dying hourly from cholera due to drinking the contaminated water.

INCREASING NATURAL DISASTERS

Whether inclement weather is blamed on El Niño or La Niña, we are barraged almost daily with news of storm-related tragedies in some distant region of the world as well as in the United States. The Weather Channel reporter has described as many as three hurricanes at once heading toward the United States. We are well aware of the recent U.S. floods, with the anguished, tearful faces of victims on the news, and in 1998 we watched far more catastrophic floods in Honduras after the worst Atlantic storm in 200 years caused torrential rains and massive mudslides. According to the First Lady of Honduras, a million people were in shelters without enough water or food, and thousands were dead or missing.

Bangladesh suffers catastrophic floods nearly every year. The flooding of the Yangzte River in China in the late summer of 1998 was the worst in over 40 years, affecting tens of millions of people and resulting in billions of dollars of lost crops.

The publication *Window Watchman II* reports that an earthquake, volcanic eruption or intense flooding is much more overwhelming in underdeveloped countries such as North Africa or China than in developed countries. Victims in such areas are more vulnerable than in developed nations for several reasons, the report states, including greater population densities; meager to non-existent warning systems; poor socioeconomic backgrounds; shabby urban construction; chronic medical illnesses; ill-equipped and often untrained response teams; inaccessible areas and inadequate technical infrastructure. In 1988, Armenia suffered a minor earthquake at midday. It leveled a city, killing 25,000 people, including all medical personnel!

During a seven-hour train ride in North Korea, we saw ruin and waste caused by severe floods. World Vision reported that the flooding in 1995 had affected 75 percent of this mountainous country, with 2,800 bridges collapsing, 100,000 homes affected and a decimated harvest that could meet only 40 percent of the need. Then, after the country was flooded again the next year, droughts later that year and in 1997 brought more devastation. Many of the collapsed bridges still had not been repaired. We inspected a large dam that provided water to hundreds of thousands of acres of land, and found the water level was 50 meters below normal and barely above the sluice gates that enabled the dam to produce hydro-electric power.

The Swedish Red Cross reported that the decades of the '60s, '70s and '80s recorded an increase in events in all categories of natural disasters: floods, storms, earthquakes, tidal waves, tornadoes, tsunamis, civil strife and accidents. The trend is continuing in the '90s, with natural calamities occurring in unsuspected places. Nashville, Tennessee, experienced its worst storm in 100 years on April 16, 1998, when twin tornadoes destroyed large downtown buildings and damaged over 300 buildings along a six-mile swath.

In 1998, Florida was not only pummeled by seven tornadoes produced by four super-cell thunderstorms, but also suffered drought and wildfires in the hottest month of June on record. In the worst fire season in 13 years, all 67 Florida counties were declared disaster areas, as 76,000 acres of Florida forest burned in three weeks.

Also in 1998, Texas and 10 other states endured severe drought. Texas farmers spent $136 million just to feed cattle, sheep and pigs because 80 percent of the hay in East Texas and 50 percent in Central Texas was lost to drought. Comparisons were made to the "Dust Bowl" of the 1930s that was centered in the Dakotas, Oklahoma and Eastern Colorado.

The July 18, 1998 issue of *U.S. News and World Report* examined the alarming possibility that global warming could cause the polar ice caps to melt, raising sea levels so much that coastal cities from New York to Los Angeles and on to Shanghai will be inundated. The key player is the West Antarctic ice sheet, a Brazil-sized mass that is as much as 7,000 feet thick and contains 90 percent of the earth's ice and 70 percent of its fresh water. If a meltdown were to occur and this vast ice sheet slid into the ocean, it would raise sea level by 20 feet worldwide, creating unparalleled consequences.

On December 31, 1998, CNN reported on a tabulation from the organization "World Watch" that shows that 1998 was the costliest year on record for natural disasters. The cost of repairing damage from such events is expected to exceed that of all the natural disasters during the entire decade of the 1980s.

THE YEAR 2000 COMPUTER BUG

Y2K, the millennium computer problem, disturbs many with its potential repercussions. Vast global computer system networks upon which our world is dependent could fail on or before January 1, 2000. Experts testifying before Congress and technological consultants agree that the problem is one of the most important issues facing us today. At times these experts seem like the prophets of old crying in the wilderness. Reactions range from disbelief and skepticism to cries of panic and catastrophe. Perhaps there will be minor disruptions; or life as we know it could change drastically for a season.

The origin of this seemingly simple problem is in the early days of mainframe computers. Space for storage of data was expensive and scarce, so computer programmers wrote lines of code using two digits for dates instead of four. For example, January 1, 1966, was written 01/01/66. These early programmers could not foresee the unbelievably widespread use of inexpensive computers with gigabytes and terabytes of space available. Nor could they foresee that the method of code writing would remain archaic, using dates based on the century 1900, compounding into millions and billions of lines of code and creating an immense tangled web to be unraveled before an unstoppable deadline.

Whatever the degree of failure, some financial and computer specialists warned in July 1998 that unless an estimated $400 to $600 billion and thousands of "person years" are dedicated immediately to correct the insidious Y2K bug, there is little hope of solving the complex problem in time to avert a calamity of unknown proportions.

There are three basic problems:

- Embedded computer chips are "burned" into computer boards that control operations on all kinds of equipment, from satellites to oil rigs. A typical oil rig in the

North Sea has 10,000 embedded chips that control the flow of oil or natural gas. (*The Millennium Bug*, by Michael Hyatt)

- We are part of a global economy. Although the English-speaking business world is aware of the problem, and many companies are diligently working to fix the Y2K bug, most of Europe's businesses are focusing instead on the conversion of its currency to the Eurodollar.
- Our computers are interlinked. A Y2K-compliant computer has checks in place to avoid processing noncompliant data. Thus there could be a communication distribution breakdown in a supply line.

Imagine a day when computer-driven air traffic is markedly diminished, communication freezes, our municipal infrastructure struggles to deliver fuel, power, water and food, and payroll and possibly welfare checks cannot be printed or delivered. (For more comprehensive information, we refer you to *Y2K: The Millennium Bug, A Balanced Christian Response* by Shaunti Feldhahn.)

The Gartner Group is the world's largest information technology (IT) research and advisory firm with more than 33,000 individual clients at more than 9,000 organizations worldwide. John Bace, research director for the Gartner Group, stated in his testimony before the Subcommittee on Oversight of the House Committee on Ways and Means on May 7, 1998:

What worries us at the Gartner Group is that as we approach New Year's Eve 1999, more and more companies will hit their Time Horizon to Failure on more and more different applications. As a result, more and more business functions within each enterprise will be negatively impacted and need to be dealt with in a crisis mode. We are afraid that there just will not be enough talent and resources available, given the amount of time left, to handle all of the potential failures in a timely fashion. As a result, companies could lose the ability to process invoices, issue payroll checks, or collect taxes for an unpredictable amount of time as they wrestle with each system failure.

Other companies who are dependent upon electronic commerce, EDI (electronic data interchange) or just-in-time manufacturing need to be concerned about the integrity of the systems of their trading partners and their supply chain. For example, the inability of a parts supplier to be able to correctly read inventory levels at a manufacturing company could shut down another firm's production line.

The result is that no single year-2000 problem hits a major artery that could kill a company. However, the combination of failures within the enterprise and from the outside might have the effect of disrupting business in such a way that the company bleeds to death instead from a series of paper cuts.

GOD'S MANDATE = YOUR DESTINY

The Church is standing on the verge of its all-time greatest opportunity in America. Why? Because people are going to be broken and hurting. In the wake of whatever disaster, when all that is familiar is torn away, humanity searches for answers. This upheaval may cause people to more seriously entertain eternity with Jesus, instead of an eternity in hell. They could be more open to the gospel than at any other time in their lives!

During the wars, earthquakes and other disturbances of the last days, "This gospel of the kingdom will be preached in the whole world as a testimony to all nations, and then the end will come" (Matt. 24:14). We are mandated by God to help redeem our own nation as well as others! The Lord is bringing this age to a powerful climax as our testimony spreads.

However, three groups in America have not responded affirmatively to the gospel:

- Those who have not heard because there has been no clear gospel presentation or witness (ethnic minorities, recent immigrants and others), especially in major cities.
- Those who have not accepted the sacrificial death of Jesus because they are turned off by counterfeit Christian messengers who live contrary to the Scriptures or present a form of godliness, denying the power.
- Those who have heard the claims of Christianity but refuse to submit to its requirements of the lordship of Jesus Christ, and thus become a god unto themselves.

The Bible clearly states that the goodness of God brings people to repentance (Rom. 2:4). What is the most loving thing that God can do? Allow sinners to go on their merry, self-gratifying way, ultimately to reside forever in a lake of fire and brimstone? Or awaken Christians to in turn awaken others to their need of a Savior and Deliverer? A gracious God shakes those priorities in our lives that need to be toppled so that what is left standing will eternally endure.

The Spirit of the Sovereign Lord is on me, because the Lord has anointed me to preach good news to the poor.

He has sent me to bind up the broken-hearted, to proclaim freedom for the captives and release from darkness for the prisoners, to proclaim the year of the Lord's favor and the day of vengeance of our God, to comfort all who mourn, and provide for those who grieve in Zion—to bestow on them a crown of beauty instead of ashes, the oil of gladness instead of mourning, and a garment of praise instead of a spirit of despair. They will be called oaks of righteousness, a planting of the Lord for the display of his splendor (Isa. 61:1-3).

Is not our destiny to equip ourselves and others to be coworkers with God in meeting the needs of people who have been awakened by times of crisis to the plight of life without God? Will you embrace this destiny? How can we partner with God to display His splendor in both the natural and spiritual realms? We, as prepared, anointed and appointed Christians can serve our communities and fellowmen to:

Rebuild the ancient ruins and restore the places long devastated; they will renew the ruined cities that have been devastated for generations . . . . And you will be called priests of the Lord, you will be named ministers of our God (Isa. 61:4,6).

THE ANATOMY OF DISASTER AND PHYSIOLOGY OF RESPONSE

BETSY NEUENSCHWANDER, M.D.

Here's a quick quiz:

1. Is your home or church near a major highway where collisions could suddenly produce toxic spills of lethal agents?
2. Is your city located in an earthquake zone?
3. Is your church near the site of a potential mass casualty event; for example, an airport or train tracks?
4. Do any of your immediate family members live near warehouses that store or utilize chemicals that might be harmful if they escaped into the atmosphere? Regardless of where you live, what would you do if terrorists released chemical or biological agents in your community?
5. Does your church leadership live near a river or dam?
6. What if the local fire, police or emergency personnel

could not react to any of these events because communications have been compromised by minor Y2K disruptions?

7. What if emergency response is diminished because worsening economic conditions have forced abrupt budget freezes and manpower layoffs?

How did you score on the above self-assessment scenarios? If believers coast to coast were polled, what do you think their scores would reveal? We have been conditioned to believe that it is the responsibility of government to respond to every crisis in our country. The government has plenty of money, logistical support and professionals trained in specialized procedures, right? It is their job? Of course! This is how its always been.

But what if these excellent agencies we depend on cannot in the future render timely help because the needs are too immense? The relief and recovery is then mandated to untrained, unprepared, ill-coordinated bystanding survivors. Would the response of these bystanders be lifesaving and damage diminishing, or would their ineptness be more life threatening and dangerous?

You're trying to scare me, you may be thinking. No, I am trying to sober you to the serious truths looming ahead. Having lived much of the last 12 years outside the high-tech, efficiency-driven U.S., I return and see a total reliance upon government service agencies for stability of our "normal lifestyle." So it is with great concern that I raise the question, what if we laity had to depend upon each other for emergency assistance?

ALERT, ALERT!

I am convicted to alert and urge the Body of Christ, collectively, to prepare for the critical times that are already upon us. Our desire is to "spur one another on toward love and good deeds" (Heb. 10:24). Think of it! A Church prudently prepared for the unexpected—aware and vigilant—quickly activating its response plan to assist survivors! Although most of the physical, nuts-and-bolts how-to's will be postponed to Section II, an overall picture of response is offered here. After all, according to Proverbs 6:10 an attitude of preparedness is a *spiritual* issue: "A little sleep, a little slumber, a little folding of the hands to rest—and poverty will come on you like a bandit and scarcity like an armed man."

Prophecies are being fulfilled in our world every day. Our Lord commands His Body, the Church, to take note of the signs of the times and position herself with plans, skills and supplies to harvest souls as she serves and blesses them.

Currently in this country, times are so good: economic buoyancy, plenty of jobs, affluence, comforts. These conditions often become stupor-inducing agents, creating spiritual and social anesthesia—as indicated in many opinion polls. Americans seem to fear disturbing the sleeping giant—for example, ignoring disasters of character, integrity and leadership in Washington. Just let things ride, don't upset the status quo lest our affluent lifestyle suffer. We need to hear John's warning:

> Do not love the world or anything in the world. If any-one loves the world, the love of the Father is not in him. For everything in the world—the cravings of sin-ful man, the lust of his eyes and the boasting of what he has and does—comes not from the Father but from the world. The world and its desires pass away, but the man who does the will of God lives forever (1 John 2:15-17).

How will our loving, merciful heavenly Father *discipline* His children? "Those whom I love I rebuke and discipline. So be earnest, and repent" (Rev. 3:19). Perhaps He may have to use the prophesied events of the last days to bring the Church to her knees and her heart to repentance.

Yes, God loves the Church, but He says we can also make Him nauseous. In Revelation 3:16,17, the original Greek describes lukewarmness as eliciting a vomit reflex in the Creator of the universe, for He says:

> Because thou art lukewarm, and neither cold nor hot, I will spew thee out of my mouth. Because thou sayest, I am rich, and increased with goods, and have need of nothing; and knowest not that thou art wretched, and miserable, and poor, and blind, and naked (*KJV*).

DISASTER AS A FORCE FOR CHANGE

As we have seen, disasters take on many forms. Any such crisis, however, can be a powerful "vehicle for change." Frederick Cuny, 25-year veteran in disaster management, once pointed out that a disaster often brings all the basic problems in a society into focus, traumatically. Disasters have a way of highlighting inherent weaknesses in a society, he said, and frequently force us to reappraise our goals.

Because of this "precipitating" quality, disasters may bring changes in community leadership—especially if current leaders prove unable to cope with the crisis. What a monumental opportunity for believers to be trained, poised and ready to emerge as servant-leaders in our communities! If a disaster presents a new window of opportunity for light to dispel darkness, we must seize the moment. Otherwise, the window will close while uninformed, untrained, yet well-meaning hearts stumble and fumble amid the chaos and pressure of a crisis event.

PREPARATION AND RESPONSE: AN OVERVIEW

Now, with these motivational building blocks, let us plunge into dissecting the anatomy of a disaster. Even though different authors use varied terms, in secular disaster management literature three to five phrases are repeatedly highlighted. It seems practical to divide an event into five phases that evolve over time. Although this chapter will focus on Phases II and III, preparation and response, it should help to have all five phases before us. The following is adapted for Christian use from secular disaster management literature.[1]

I. Mitigation (pre-event phase)
   A. Investigate potential, natural or possible man-made disasters of region.
   B. Analyze them and determine action steps to prevent or reduce impact.
   C. Activate these minimizing procedures.
   D. Promote public awareness.
   E. Minister faith and hope to the fearful.
II. Preparedness (pre-event)
   A. Recruit and train workers.
   B. Construct and practice response plan.
   C. Procure, stock and maintain supplies.
   D. Pray redemptively, enlisting intercessors and "praise warriors" (see Ps. 149:6-9; Isa. 61:3).

—IMPACT! DISASTER EVENT—

III. Relief/Response (acute phase; may last hours or weeks)

    A. Rapidly deploy advance scout team (official, pre-trained workers)

    B. Stabilize incident.

    C. Assess and plan (evaluate scope of the event, determine and secure safety of workers, then activate the plan).

    D. Utilize Incident Command System (see p. 89).

    E. Apply triage strategies ("triage" means "to sort"):

        1. Event triage: assess problems and match workers' skills with needs and locales.

        2. Victim triage: prioritize injuries/needs for therapeutic treatment.

    F. Recruit and assign additional workers.

    G. Periodically reassess and systematically alter protocols as warranted.

    H. Serve and minister.

IV. Rehabilitation (acute phase transitioning to chronic; may last months or years)

    A. Assess, then activate, strategic plans (i.e., rebuild homes)

    B. Recruit workers with specialties and supplies to repair damage.

    C. Serve, witness, disciple, initiate cell churches.

V. Reconstruction/Restoration (restoring normalcy and productivity; may last weeks, months or years)

    A. Assess and create strategic plan (i.e., reestablishing businesses and community lifestyle).

    B. Recruit and deploy workers and raw materials.

    C. Continue to serve, witness and make disciples, multiplying cell church network.

With this overall schematic before us, let's go into more detail, with special emphasis on Phases II and III.

PHASE I—MITIGATION

Mitigation is a predisaster period during which steps are deliberately taken to reduce the force or intensity of a potential or anticipated disaster. A practical example of mitigating a disaster is building a levee along a vulnerable river bank to reduce the force of flooding, and thus minimize its damage to lives and property. Another example is spending millions of dollars and personnel hours becoming Y2K compliant (with successful testing) before the summer of 1999.

An explicit biblical prototype of this principle is Joseph's grain project, which served to mitigate the effect of the Middle East's drought of Genesis 41. Hindrances to the effectiveness of this phase include underestimating the risk, inadequate awareness, overreliance on technology, denial and fatalism.

PHASE II—PREPAREDNESS

Obstacles to the preparedness phase include the hindrances listed above, plus indifference, preoccupation with other priorities and neglecting to allocate funds.

GOD'S EARLY WARNING SYSTEM
In order to prepare, one needs first to have some idea of what is coming. Does God have an early warning system?

> When a trumpet sounds in a city, do not the people tremble? When disaster comes to a city, has not the Lord

caused it? Surely the Sovereign Lord does nothing without revealing his plan to his servants the prophets
(Amos 3:6,7).

The secret things belong to the Lord our God, but the
things revealed belong to us and to our children forever,
that we may follow all the words of this law (Deut. 29:29).

During this time some prophets came down from
Jerusalem to Antioch. One of them, named Agabus, stood
up and through the Spirit predicted that a severe famine
would spread over the entire Roman world. The disciples,
each according to his ability, decided to provide help for
the brothers living in Judea. This they did, sending their
gift to the elders by Barnabas and Saul (Acts 11:27-30).

I think it is impressive that with *only* the prophet's prediction,
believers immediately took up an offering to help *before* the famine
actually occurred! They did not wait for confirmation from the
national weathermen. Note also that Paul, who wrote "My God will
meet all your needs" (Phil. 4:19), also wrote, "I have labored and
toiled and have often gone without sleep; I have known hunger and
thirst and have often gone without food; I have been cold and
naked" (2 Cor. 11:27). This is the man who organized the relief
effort for the famine prophesied by Agabus!

As children in Sunday School we learned of God-directed preparedness for global flooding in Genesis 6–9. We read of the
ridicule Noah experienced; his perseverance through decades of
the ark's construction; and the loneliness of obedience he suffered
to save a remnant. How does one balance these biblical relief
epics of futuristic preparation with "So do not worry, saying,

'What shall we eat?' or 'What shall we drink?' or 'What shall we wear?' ... But seek first his kingdom and his righteousness, and all these things will be given to you as well" (Matt. 6:31,33)?

I believe the answer is found in the context of the motive for our "worrying." Look at Matthew 6:19-21,25:

> Do not store up for yourselves treasures on earth, where moth and rust destroy, and where thieves break in and steal. But store up for yourselves treasures in heaven, where moth and rust do not destroy, and where thieves do not break in and steal. For where your treasure is, there your heart will be also .... Therefore I tell you, do not worry about your life, what you will eat or drink; or about your body, what you will wear.

The warning here seems to be against preparation that is driven by *self-centered worry*. On the other hand, if our motive is to store up "treasures in heaven," this could be maximized by acts of faithful, unselfish preparation. The "treasure" we desire is to bless more souls; hence to collect supplies in preparation for a disaster, *acquiring more to give more*, is seeking first the Kingdom.

Some may reply, "Don't bother me! I have faith that God can even feed us with ravens, as He did for Elijah." They're right; He might have to, after all our supplies are dispersed! Can you—will you—really act at that level of faith? Can your faith level believe God for enough ravens to feed your whole neighborhood or suburb?

DEVELOP THE PREPAREDNESS PLAN

Is a landslide in a deserted canyon a disaster? Certainly not. When sculpting your church's strategy for ministry in crisis, insightful planning will be required. Careful analysis of the potential hazards in your region will help expose your community's unique vulnerability.

Next, weigh various disaster risks against available resources. For instance, in a rural community hospital a 10-victim highway accident could be overwhelming, definitely a calamitous event. However, this is a regular occurrence at large urban trauma centers where a large number of patients can be more easily managed. A good question to ask is: Can the severity of estimated injuries and property damage be handled through routine procedures and with the existing work force and material supplies?

What useful data should be gathered to evaluate hazards with corresponding response capabilities? Key areas to examine are *characteristics of the hazard, duration of former occurrences, anticipated severity* and *frequency of impact.* Let's hypothesize briefly.

In considering natural disasters, remember that they will be, by definition, geographically self-contained, thereby allowing aid to be brought in from areas of normalcy. However, if the Y2K problem, for example, results in simultaneous, diffuse, massive disruptions (even if only technologically minor), there could be few areas of non-impact from which to dispatch reinforcement. If Y2K is only a "speed bump," as many Christian leaders suppose, then could great trauma strike instead from global financial collapse?

We were on the soil when the Korean *won* plummeted, Malaysia's *ringet* was devalued and the Russian *ruble's* worth almost evaporated. How will Americans, most of whom live on the financial edge (with less than two months' cash reserves), act if the value of the dollar plunges overnight and remains depressed? This man-made disaster could initiate a run on banks, rioting, stealing, escalated violence, hunger, exposure and worsening of chronic medical conditions—since there would be little money for medications, procedures, etc.

What is the degree of probable loss (health, property, life, etc.) per person posed by such scenarios, whether singly or superimposed upon each other? I am not an economist or financial expert, but I strongly believe that a global financial calamity is inevitable. Remember: It wasn't raining when Noah started building his ship! I do not know the time frame, but at this writing we are witnessing large oil company mergers, Boeing Airlines employee reductions and massive layoffs in Fortune 500 companies. I have to wonder whether this is all symptom driven, or if business leaders in high places have an economic radar that forecasts turmoil.

After a critical study of plausible natural and man-made hazards in your region, it is imperative to survey the response assets currently available (human, material, etc.) to see if they equal the risk. If the resources are markedly lower, the result is a deficit, or unmet needs. *The magnitude of suffering can be predicted in proportion to unmet needs.* These concepts can enhance the efficient formulation of your own customized protocol.

In his previously referenced work, disaster management expert Dr. Auf der Heide writes:

A disaster triggers the mobilization of people trying to do quickly what they do not ordinarily do, further complicated by an unfamiliar environment. What was previously the private sector is thrust alongside government agencies into critical working conditions. Unfortunately, since they have often planned independently, they respond independently, each having little grasp of how the other fits into the overall effort.

Dr. Auf der Heide's description can be negated by you and your church's preliminary study and training! Rehearsing plans allow such help to be an asset instead of a liability in the fast-paced response.

SKELETON OF THE PLAN

To amplify this preparation phase section, refer to the Incident Command System flow chart as the skeleton for your planning.[2] Further elaboration and practical application will follow later in this book. We believe that this model will augment your ministry deployment, and we encourage you to learn and use it.

Since most U.S. municipalities employ this same structure, your congregation can be integrated more smoothly into "serving the servers" of your community during acute crisis. Helpful hearts will be a greater glory to Jesus when they are accompanied by the "homework" of understanding this protocol's functions and sequencing. Instead of requiring detailed, lengthy explanations during an emergency, your volunteer church members will know what to do during life-saving interventions, and their efforts will flow smoothly and competently alongside the city's paid professional responders.

Now, let's look more closely at the Incident Command System, which directs government response activities in most communities. The plan is based on the general concepts of *management by objectives* (like business models) from the book *Disaster Response* by Erik Auf der Heide, M.D., and employs *functional clarity* while maintaining *specialized unit integrity*. Other unique features include an *effective span of control*—each leader being responsible for only three to five (occasionally seven) personnel. Thus in the chaotic, sudden nature of crises, formal lines of communication are compressed and tight. Especially appealing is the use of common

INCIDENT COMMAND SYSTEM

Incident Commander

Staging Manager

Personal Staff: Outside Liaison, Press Relations, Safety Officer (Command center, retrieval site, hospital, supply depots)

Operations

Damage Assessment & Repair

Fire & Hazardous Materials Services

Victim Search & Rescue

Field Medical Triage

Patient Tracking

Field Hospital/Clinic

Victim Services

Food, water, clothing, shelter, orphanage, mortuary, spiritual counseling for victims, families & children

Responders' Base Camp

Power, water, maintenance, sanitation, dining, Team's spiritual, emotional, physical well-being

Logistics

Communications (internal, external) Equipment & Maintenance

Supplies Procurement Storage & Tracking

Transportation & Maintenance

Planning

Incident Information Retrieval, Analysis

Develop Plans, then Communicate

Ongoing Planning

Modify Plans

Recommunicate

Recycle Process

Finance

Develop Budget

Expenses Authorized

Bookkeeping

Accounting

Submit Reports

Treasurer

terminology so that different groups within a city's response team or those arriving from adjacent states can work a homogeneous plan with greater proficiency.

Finally, the *modular configuration* with tiered branching permits expanding and contracting the work force in sync with various evolving phases of crisis intervention. Also, the basic categories can be modified to address several kinds of emergencies.

Look specifically at each major area. At the top, the "Incident Commander" with staff is to organize and manage the entire crisis response by establishing objectives that will stabilize the incident and save life and property. Such persons set goals and determine priorities for accomplishing tasks. They are responsible for the ongoing development of rudimentary action plans, receiving hourly updates on all aspects of the event. With constant assessments of incoming data, Incident Command authorizes and directs all other divisions.

Note that immediately beneath the *commander* is a *safety officer* and a *liaison officer.* The safety officer protects the command post and its personnel, establishes an evacuation plan for the entire team as well as for casualties and provides protection of supplies from looting, sabotage, etc. The liaison officer interfaces with other organizations.

Before we note the four horizontal categories heading the vertical columns, observe the label *Staging Manager.* This person supervises the assembling of trained and untrained volunteers, assesses their skills and assigns them to the most current critically relevant positions. This checkpoint prevents premature or inadequate deployment of manpower and supplies. It also precludes unsupervised activity amid the chaos.

Now on to the four main "work horses" of the endeavor. *Operations* implements the plan to achieve the tactical objectives.

Logistics provides support services for operations to achieve objectives expeditiously. They procure and track all human, technical and mechanical resources for the team and for survivors/victims.

Planning helps the *safety officer* create the evacuation strategy, continuously gathers data and analyzes the status of the event (i.e., initial earthquake followed by fires due to broken gas mains, with additional damage from aftershocks). Planning advisors (technical specialists) formulate and distribute comprehensive action plans, estimate future probable complications within the emergency, then devise contingency strategies for managing additional dilemmas.

Finance develops a budget, authorizes expenditures; contracts with vendors; tracks time or use of rental equipment; keeps personnel records and time cards; and maintains accounting and bookkeeping records.

CREATING YOUR DISASTER/EVANGELISM TASK FORCE

The effectiveness of your preparation for responding to a disaster revolves around the creation of a Disaster/Evangelism Task Force. This will require surveying your local congregation and compiling a resource directory. If your church is small, partner with a larger congregation or coalesce several small churches for depth of manpower needs, etc. The following list can "jumpstart" the process.

I. Manpower

public works personnel	security people
mobile canteen/caterer	pharmacists
retail grocers	EMTs
restaurant owners	firefighters
chefs	mental health counselors

mechanics
electricians
plumbers
engineers (all specialties)
chain-saw operators
administrators
computer personnel
data processors
bookkeepers
accountants
fuel suppliers
transportation
   providers and drivers
   (cars and trucks, RV's,
   four-wheel-drive
   vehicles
language translators
signers for hearing
hazardous materials
   specialists
doctors
nurses

dentists
veterinarians
wilderness survival
   specialists
facility managers
custodial caretakers for
   shelters
communications
   technicians
ham radio operators
pastoral care staff
children's evangelistic
   ministry teams
praise and worship teams
intercessors

II. Materials
A. Communications
1. Choose alternatives to normal telephone
2. Obtain stash of coins for pay phones, with a pre arranged system for personnel to initiate strategically networked communications
3. CB radios, 2-way radios with extra batteries, ham radios, fax, police scanner, cell phones, copy

machine, E-mail set-up (with preset address list for immediate notification)
4. predesigned logistical forms
5. preprinted signs
6. maps of districts and zones, traffic and victim flow, base camp facilities, triage area, morgue, etc.

B. Response team supplies
1. category-labeled personnel vests
2. patient triage tags (clinical conditions of severity)
3. barricade tape
4. signs for labeling building structures
5. sandbags
6. hard hats
7. flashlights with spare batteries
8. tool sets
9. ropes
10. duct tape (copious amounts)
11. advance team's hazardous materials gear, including medical items
12. search and rescue supplies
13. medical tent supplies
14. command post items (pens, markers, computers, maps, wall-chart rosters, communications equipment, etc.)
15. shelter facilities with food/water and around-the-clock counseling

C. Fundamental victim services
1. purified water
2. food with utensils
3. shelter
4. blankets

5. sanitation (latrines, showers, soap, toilet paper)
6. alternative energy source with fuels for heat/lights for all above facilities and functions
7. victim tracking services and counseling

D. Alternative shelter/ministry sites

1. church facilities with preassigned service zones delineated with traffic patterns
2. designated section leaders predetermined and marked access route to supply materials with disbursement system, etc.
3. other possible sites to consider: nearby skating rink, parking garage, empty warehouse, recreational facility, hotel ballroom, school, college/university, park, campground

E. Prestored ministry supplies

1. cell-church manuals
2. Bibles (in multiple languages if appropriate for your population mix)
3. discipleship literature—fundamentals of faith, i.e., *Firm Foundations* by Bob and Rose Weiner
4. booklets on hope, faith, God's character, comfort, healing, loss
5. children's Bibles, literature, toys, songs, videos (with players)
6. praise & worship music tapes, CDs with player
7. games—adult and children's
8. crafts—adult and children's

F. Construct basic record forms (or procure from fire department/FEMA)

1. "roll-call" notification registry for responders (with their skills)

2. organization chart (Incident Command Diagram)
3. comprehensive personnel assignment directory (including names for leaders of all sections, divisions, branches, etc., with deputies/assistants, etc.
4. staging check-in list (date, time, name, skills, where assigned)
5. personnel roster with time sheets for each subdivision
6. warehouse/supplies/inventory catalogues, including items, expiration date, date received, ID no., dispersed to _____, by _____, etc.
7. task objectives work sheet (problems, work assigned, resources required, on-hand, requisitioned/ETA, etc.)

The preceding lists are certainly not exhaustive, but should stimulate your creative thinking. Each section can also generate its own documents relevant to its unique function. For example, the medical division (under operations) would format abbreviated patient charts or "short forms."

PRACTICE DRILL

This part is really fun! Great interest and enthusiasm can infect your church or city's ministerial association if you involve them in an enactment of a disaster event for practicing unified efficient response. Two options are possible. First and less expensive is a "tabletop" mock disaster.

After your leadership team has produced your customized disaster evangelism plan that addresses several probable scenarios (i.e., regional natural disaster, moderate Y2K disruptions of utilities, food supplies, payroll, etc.), then schedule a pretend indoors "tabletop" event to practice your strategy logistically. Here's how:

Write beforehand a narrative of the impacting hazard with details and multiple evolving complications. Put the five basic leadership areas (Incident Command, Operations, etc.) in different rooms with walkie-talkies and let participants in each division problem-solve cohesively. It's really a blast for the next two hours!

Several months after you have successfully completed this exercise amid cheers of glee and victory, stage a drill with "mock victims" (volunteers hopefully from your church, youth group, home schoolers). Physically set up the Incident Command, Staging Area, Victim Triage, Supply Warehouse, etc. Write another scenario, with looting and secondary explosive sabotage woven into the major catastrophe. Arrange for the ketchup-covered "wounded" to be scattered over an area that is at least one-half mile in diameter. This outdoor exercise is great to involve entire ministerial associations. The excitement may woo other spiritual leaders to get more involved for actual realistic and unified response. Then you can realize the intent of Proverbs 24:11,12:

> Rescue those being led away to death; hold back those staggering toward slaughter. If you say, "But we knew nothing about this," does not he who weighs the heart perceive it? Does not he who guards your life know it? Will he not repay each person according to what he has done?

If you want more coaching in originating an outdoor mock disaster, we have video footage of mock incidents, as well as video instruction for creating simulated wounds. Better still, just come to our training courses! Live it firsthand! (For videos or a schedule of training events, contact: International Health Services Foundation, P. O. Box 49536, Colorado Springs, CO 80949-9536. E-mail: ihsf@aol.com. Tel.: 719-481-1379. Fax: 719-481-1378.)

This brief overview of a standard schematic for managing a disaster will hopefully expedite your own response design.

PHASE III—RELIEF/RESPONSE

Your life-saving response will be straightforward and synchronized if a preliminary plan has been constructed and practiced with mock drills, and if supplies are stockpiled. If, however, prudence has not produced the above deployment readiness, critical minutes, hours and unfortunately days can rapidly steal lives and property!

The first 24 hours is considered the most critical window for victim retrieval with survivability. After 72 hours almost no casualties are extricated alive. If paid professional disaster personnel cannot be on the scene for whatever reason, then loss of life and property would be markedly reduced if lay persons were trained and available. These workers need to possess basic knowledge of emergency protocols, accompanied by technical skills.

One of the Church's greatest evangelistic opportunities is to systematically, competently, efficaciously and compassionately distribute aid, solace and hope to masses of people who are paralyzed by shock, trapped under rubble, hemorrhaging profusely or overcome with grief. That level of preparation, however, requires an investment of time, energy, resources and selfless risk. Is the Church willing to pay that price? We should again reflect on Paul's statement about Christ, who "died for all, that those who live should no longer live for themselves but for Him who died for them and was raised again" (2 Cor. 5:15).

In the initial minutes of response, while the Incident Command Post is being assembled, an advance party is rapidly deployed to quickly ascertain: (1) physical data—weather, wind direction, terrain, etc.; (2) the magnitude of damage, types and scope of injuries and other acute needs; (3) the status of local resources; (4) known and postulated potential risks, secondary hazards, obstacles to recovery efforts, etc.

Maps of the site itself, with ancillary maps for water, gas mains and other hazardous locales, plus a map of the forming base camp are quickly produced or procured. Rosters of available personnel, categorized by skill and geographical distribution, are activated. Inventories of prestocked supplies are surveyed and coordinated with subsequent mobilization of other appropriate materials. Logistics swiftly activates the preplanned communication system (alternatives to telephones, which, even if they're in working order, are often overloaded).

Transportation of supplies commences over prior assigned routes to designated distribution points (churches or home cell groups are excellent!). Warehousing personnel have previously inventoried supplies, included packing lists; rotated date-dependent items; and monitored climate or rodent damage. They can now dispense stocked items with predesigned tracking forms. As dispersal occurs logistics officers monitor consumption, anticipate early reorder and provide maintenance on vehicles delivering the precious cargo.

BRINGING ORDER FROM CHAOS

The fundamental, universal tenets in disaster management are to bring order to chaos as rapidly as possible; stabilize the incident; assess and monitor secondary risks; and save lives and property.

The efficiency with which you and your team bring order

and relief on a mass scale is in direct proportion to the level of your preparedness. It all depends on:

1. Sufficient personnel, who have "austere event" training and competent skill levels.
2. Prestocked, accessible, relevant supplies in adequate volume.
3. A timely, organized response pattern.

Doesn't that make sense? If you race to the emergency room with your loved one and find that everyone on duty just graduated yesterday from medical and nursing school, how confident do you feel in a life/death situation? Again I ask: If the government-paid disaster professional cannot respond adequately for whatever reason, should not the Church, the Body of the Great Physician, have invested the extra time, money and expertise to marshal its inherent skilled "member resources" for ministering help, hope and salvation? Wouldn't this supremely demonstrate His glory?

Contrariwise, little or no spiritual or natural preparation (supplies, manpower, coherent plan) results in spastic, chaotic relief attempts in a vortex of pandemonium!

In actual disasters, an advance team composed of hazardous materials experts, emergency health-care personnel, civil structural engineers and logisticians is rapidly deployed to speedily determine the nature and scope of the calamity; numbers and locale of affected people; percentage of women, children, elderly and disabled; nature and severity of injuries; whether conditions are safe for deployment of the entire response team (i.e., no hazardous agents detected, low risk of secondary sabotage or probability of aftershocks).

The team determines the most critical needs. This information is expeditiously relayed to Incident Command. A specific plan (including immediate evacuation strategies) is activated from prior generic protocols, then communicated to designated personnel who commence particular tasks (hazard remediation, search and rescue, triage). Meanwhile, a base camp is established, with safe water, sanitation and food for team and survivors.

RESPONDING TO PARTICULAR CRISES

Response will vary somewhat depending on the unique aspects of particular calamities. Hopefully the following overview will broaden the scope of your understanding, hence planning.

Earthquakes. In earthquakes, gas mains are fractured, giving rise to fires. Plus, we see entrapment, crush and neurological injuries. Respiratory problems from dust inhalation are also common. The civil engineering structures of water supply, purification, waste water and solid waste plants are damaged. Epidemic infectious diseases then result from this contamination. Other critical features often include power outages and blocked rescue routes (creating more exposure and delayed treatment of injuries). All these contingencies require multifactor problem solving.

Floods. Factors affecting response to floods include evacuating or rescuing people from virtually inaccessible areas as well as the obstruction of incoming aid by high water. Water sources usually become contaminated, producing epidemic diarrheal illnesses within the compromised populace. The drowning of humans, animals and crops enhances vector-borne diseases from the decay. Characteristic injuries are impalements, lacerations and hypothermia. Power and communication are commonly damaged. Electrocution occurs from downed lines in standing water.

Windstorms. Tornadoes and hurricanes commonly destroy

power sources and other building structures, creating diverse traumatic injuries. Response routes are usually blocked by debris, thus delaying and complicating emergency care.

Note the similarities between contingency measures needed after natural disasters and the preemptive steps required if Y2K disruptions occur. Computer failure could result in major delays of train-delivered foodstuffs, multiple-state power outages, clean-water shortages, ineffective communications, malfunctioning health-care equipment, inaccessible computerized prescription data, irretrievable accounting of government reimbursements and the banking industry's cash shortage. Many of these problems could spawn violence, resulting in multiple casualties. So the same preparatory steps are useful in a variety of potential crises.

PHASE IV—REHABILITATION

Rehabilitation follows acute relief/response. The initial steps are cleanup, repair and steps to return individuals and their communities to preimpact lifestyles. In this phase, media coverage and excessive flow of manpower and supplies has now subsided. Frantic urgency has abated, replaced by the methodical and systematic rebuilding of infrastructure, dwellings, families, businesses and lives.

Post-traumatic stress disorder can manifest itself now, if it hasn't already. Care-givers should be trained to diagnose and treat this clinical condition, which can progress from depression to incapacitation. Responders as well as victims are subject to this psychological disorder. Diligent, consistent effort must be made to (1) pre-brief responders with Scripture, prayer, praise, etc.; (2) debrief responders who have been forced to process so much death, destruction and sorrow that they become overwhelmed; plus (3) debrief and counsel survivors and their families.

In addition to depression, symptoms may include sleep difficulties, tenseness, shakiness, digestive problems and/or sexual dysfunction. Emotional reactions include feeling insulated from the world, forgetting that there were any pleasurable experiences before the trauma, irritability, being easily startled, guilt stemming from having survived while loved ones perished and memory dullness or even loss.

Pastoral ministry for team members is as vital as for adult and pediatric victims. We believe intercessors and praise/worshipers on site in the response and rehabilitation phases are paramount. See how easily discipleship can be a natural outgrowth of disaster relief?

PHASE V—RECONSTRUCTION/RESTORATION

The concluding phase, reconstruction or restoration, returns the populace to full normalcy and productivity. Processes initiated in the rehabilitation phase are completed over weeks, months or possibly years, depending on the nature of the catastrophe. In this important phase, discipleship in a cell church model should be employed (see chapter 5).

TAKING JESUS SERIOUSLY
Jesus' predictions of the last days are looming upon the horizon. He warned that:

> "Nation will rise against nation, and kingdom against kingdom. There will be famines and earthquakes in various places. All these are the beginning of birth pains.

Then you will be handed over to be persecuted and put to death, and you will be hated by all nations because of me. At that time many will turn away from the faith and will betray and hate each other, and many false prophets will appear and deceive many people. Because of the increase of wickedness, the love of most will grow cold, but he who stands firm to the end will be saved" (Matt. 24:7-13).

It seems prudent for us to take our cues from Christ and become poised to utilize tragic events to maximize His deepest desire: that none should perish but all come to the knowledge of Him (2 Pet. 3:9). If we fail to do so, what will be our excuses? Is it that we are too busy with jobs, families, kids and church activities, with no time or money left over to undertake Christian disaster evangelism? Also, we assume that the National Guard, FEMA or Civil Defense personnel will do it, right? But as helpful as these agencies are, they do not offer rescue from the greatest disaster of the universe—eternity in hell. People often come to Christ in crisis because their shallow, false foundations are in rubble. They need extrication from the kingdom of darkness into the Kingdom of light!

If you went to heaven two hours after you close the pages of this book, how many people would be there because of your life and active witness? Just estimate. Of course none of us is totally aware of the subtle eternal influences we have had on people. But are you satisfied with the number you just calculated? Do you think millions in our country need to know personally the God who sacrificially experienced Calvary's trauma for *each* of them? Who else will tell them if you and I do not, will not, cannot? Are dreadful events opportunities for the Body of Christ to do what the Head died for? Let's act!

I hope that taking Jesus seriously will make you want to proceed to the next chapters on crisis evangelism.

Notes

1. See especially *Disaster Response: Principles of Preparation and Coordination*, by Erik Auf der Heide, M.D. (St. Louis: C. V. Mosby Co., 1989).

2. We have modified this administrative configuration from material presented in a course conducted by the Oklahoma City Fire Department. The original Incident Command System was developed by California fire fighters and is now taught at the National Fire Academy and also utilized by the Federal Emergency Management Administration (FEMA) and the National Disaster Medical System (NDMS) teams in federal deployment.

CRISIS EVANGELISM: PRINCIPLES AND EXAMPLES

BETSY NEUENSCHWANDER, M.D.

Did you hear about or see the movie *Schindler's List*? As it draws to a close, the image of hundreds of Jewish people fills the big screen. With obvious emotion, choking back the tears, they present a German man (probably not a believer) with a token of appreciation—a gold ring forged from a few milligrams of gold retrieved from their sacrificially extracted teeth (without anesthesia!). In the moonlight as Schindler, the German, takes the ring, he begins to weep, saying (in my paraphrase), "I could have saved more. I could have saved them. Why didn't I? I lived wasting so much money."

The Jewish spokesman for the large group tries to console him: "But you saved so many—here we are." The tall recipient then slumps into the Hebrew's arms, crumpling under the emotional weight . . . realizing that more people could be alive if he had made different choices, different value judgments.

Collecting himself, he stands and slowly moves to his car, mumbling, "Why did I keep this car? I could have saved almost a dozen more people with its value." Pausing, he fumbles with the lapel of his suit coat, stripping from it a pin. "Gold—I could have saved a couple . . . or at least one more, but . . . I didn't, I didn't." He sobs with gut-wrenching regret. A few frames later the entire breadth of the screen is filled with survivors linked arm in arm, walking toward us, the audience. The scene dissolves into the real-life stream of over 6,000 descendants living today because an ordinary man risked and sacrificed amid a man-made disaster—World War II and the Jewish holocaust!

We show the final moments of this film in our training schools because it so powerfully depicts what we believe should throb daily in the spirits of all Christians. One day, how many will fill heaven's portals because of your life of commitment, selflessness and ministry of compassion?

THE DIVINE SEARCH AND RESCUE TEAM

The greatest Search and Rescue Team of the universe is God the Father, Son and Holy Spirit, because God so loved the world that He gave His only Son.

The German businessman Oskar Schindler, who risked his life to save Jews, *lived* 1 John 3:16: "This is how we know what love is: Jesus Christ laid down his life for us. And we ought to lay down our lives for our brothers." The qualities of these spiritual genes are transferred to us when we are "born again," for John continues in verses 17 and 18: "If anyone has material possessions and sees his brother in need but has no pity on him, how can the love of God be in him? Dear children, let us not love with words or tongue but with actions and in truth."

In our bustling, economically robust society, what are the lifestyle indicators that demonstrate that the Church believes the greatest disaster is spending eternity in hell? Is John 14:6 an absolute? "I am the way and the truth and the life. No one comes to the Father except through me [Jesus]." Note that "me" is a personal pronoun, not a doctrine, creed or denomination.

I think that the apostle Paul was fully persuaded that Jesus' statement was an absolute—"I pray that you may be active in sharing your faith" (Philem. 6). "Though I am free and belong to no man, I make myself a *slave to everyone, to win as many as possible*" (1 Cor. 9:19, author's emphasis), "so that the grace that is *reaching more and more people* may cause thanksgiving to overflow to the glory of God" (2 Cor. 4:15, author's emphasis). Paul's passion for people stimulates me!

Before investigating the specialized aspects of evangelism during a crisis, maybe we should reexamine *the fundamental evangelistic mandate from Jesus* as recorded in the concluding verses of Matthew, Mark, Luke and John.

When they saw him, they worshiped him; but some doubted. Then Jesus came to them and said, "All authority in heaven and on earth has been given to me. Therefore go and make disciples [trained ones] of all nations, baptizing them in the name of the Father and of the Son and of the Holy Spirit, and teaching them to obey everything I have commanded you. And surely I am with you always, to the very end of the age" (Matt. 28:17-20).

He said to them, "Go into all the world and preach the good news to all creation. Whoever believes and is baptized will be saved, but whoever does not believe will be condemned. And these signs will accompany those who believe: In my name they will drive out demons; they will speak in new tongues; they will pick up snakes with their hands; and when they drink deadly poison, it will not hurt them at all; they will place their hands on sick people, and they will get well." After the Lord Jesus had spoken to them, he was taken up into heaven and he sat at the right hand of God. Then the disciples went out and preached everywhere, and the Lord worked with them and confirmed his word by the signs that accompanied it (Mark 16:15-20).

"You are witnesses of these things. I am going to send you what my Father has promised; but stay in the city until you have been clothed with power from on high" (Luke 24:48,49).

When they had finished eating, Jesus said to Simon Peter, "Simon son of John, do you truly love me more than these?" "Yes, Lord," he said, "you know that I love you." Jesus said, "Feed my lambs." Again Jesus said, "Simon son of John, do you truly love me?" He answered, "Yes, Lord, you know that I love you." Jesus said, "Take care of my sheep." The third time he said to him, "Simon son of John, do you love me?" Peter was hurt because Jesus asked him the third time, "Do you love me?" He said, "Lord, you know all things; you know that I love you." Jesus said, "Feed my sheep" (John 21:15-17).

Whether we have just recently been born again or have been a Christian for years, our mandate is to spread the good news. If search and rescue was important enough for Father God to sacrifice His child, then His heart must be our heart—for the servant is not greater than the master, Jesus declared (see Matt.

10:24). Evangelism based on the essence of Jesus' principles from these four passages is straightforward and simple:

1. GO preach good news in the midst of bad news (crises) and baptize new believers.
2. GO with delegated authority and make trained ones, teaching them to obey everything I commanded you.
3. BE CLOTHED with power, and demonstrate signs in Jesus' name: healings, exorcisms, etc.
4. FEED My lambs and sheep because you love them out of your love for Me, their Shepherd, Jesus.

The book of Acts further describes being clothed with power:

For John baptized with water, but in a few days you will be baptized with the Holy Spirit.... But you will receive power when the Holy Spirit comes on you; and you will be my witnesses in Jerusalem, and in all Judea and Samaria, and to the ends of the earth (Acts 1:5,8).

When the day of Pentecost came, they were all together in one place. Suddenly a sound like the blowing of a violent wind came from heaven and filled the whole house where they were sitting. They saw what seemed to be tongues of fire that separated and came to rest on each of them. All of them were filled with the Holy Spirit and began to speak in other tongues as the Spirit enabled them. Now there were staying in Jerusalem God-fearing Jews from every nation under heaven. When they heard this sound, a crowd came together in bewilderment, because each one heard them speaking in his own language. Utterly amazed, they asked: "Are not all these men who are speaking Galileans? Then how is it that each of us hears them in his own native language? Parthians, Medes and Elamites; residents of Mesopotamia, Judea and Cappadocia, Pontus and Asia, Phrygia and Pamphylia, Egypt and the parts of Libya near Cyrene; visitors from Rome (both Jews and converts to Judaism); Cretans and Arabs—we hear them declaring the wonders of God in our own tongues!" (Acts 2:1-11).

Oh, what awesome truths! Look at the diverse, numerous nationalities impacted with God's sovereign power, in verses 9 to 11! Wow! These concepts are the reason God pours out the presence and power of His Spirit, "the anointing"—*to help people!* In fact, you recall in Luke 4:18, His first sermon, that the Great Physician, Jesus, quotes Isaiah's words:

The Spirit of the Lord is on me, because he has anointed me to preach good news to the poor. He has sent me to proclaim freedom for the prisoners and recovery of sight for the blind, to release the oppressed, to proclaim the year of the LORD'S favor (Isa. 61:1,2).

And in John 10:10 we find His reassuring words: "The thief comes only to steal and kill and destroy; I have come that they may have life, and have it to the full."

EVANGELISM IN CRISIS—JESUS' PLAN

Free the captives! Bind up the brokenhearted! Release prisoners from darkness! Not only does Jesus tell us to share faith in Him;

He tells us to help make their lives better. When there is a catastrophe, we have been commissioned by God Himself, in Isaiah 61 and Luke 4, to get involved.

Can you see how Jesus' evangelistic mandate fits into disasters? His commands fit precisely into the five phases of disaster anatomy outlined in chapter 4. Below are His tenets summarized and matched with phases of a disaster:

Phase I—Mitigation: Wait for the promise, power from on high (to mitigate the force of the disaster's impact).

Phase II—Preparedness: Be adequately trained in order to train (i.e., make disciples).

Phase III—Relief/Response: Go preach the good news under His almighty authority, demonstrating miraculous signs (which are especially vital in a mass catastrophe).

Phase IV—Rehabilitation: Baptize, teach and train (as we help restore).

Phase V—Reconstruction/Restoration: Provide pastures (safe perimeters, food, water, etc.) for long-term feeding of His precious lambs and sheep.

How have others evangelized in these five phases? Read with delight, esteem and praise the following graphic testimonies (separated to exemplify the phases of disaster response) from our Disaster Training graduates and/or faculty. They are beautiful, awe-inspiring examples of God's heart in action. These folks were salt and light!

PHASE I—EVANGELIZING IN THE MITIGATION PHASE

You recall that mitigation means performing steps in anticipation of a calamity to reduce potential damage and casualties—for example, cities along the Mississippi build levees in advance to prevent the rising river from flooding their homes and businesses.

You can reduce harm, injury and even death as we transition the 21st century! You can provide civic public awareness, then teach preventative procedures for specific potential disasters.

For example, Shaunti Feldhahn has written a book in anticipation of a Y2K crisis, desiring to reduce its damage by forewarning, then offering solutions for mitigation. Her book *Y2K: The Millennium Bug, A Balanced Christian Response* began to alert people 14 months before "impact." It presents practical strategies to reduce or "mitigate" the possible discomfort that could be inflicted upon businesses, ministries and families. Readers who follow her advice can facilitate *preemptive modification* of their lifestyles to compensate for later unpreventable (by the time line) disruptions caused by the "millennium bug." While heralding mitigation, the author is also enthusiastically calling the Church to awareness of her finest hour: opportunities for servant ministry, evangelism and discipleship . . . in crisis.

Founding The Joseph Project 2000, Shaunti Feldhahn is equipping believers nationally to be salt and light. "Mitigation" will then manifest itself through those prepared, with wisdom and supplies, who can reduce the pain, trauma and confusion of many embroiled in Y2K municipal utilities failures, food shortages, cash-flow crises and other scenarios. *Lord, help us to be salt that preserves light in a power outage.*

Be perceptive! There are many opportunities for preimpact evangelism. Many who studiously evaluate Y2K literature become frightened, realizing their inadequacies. Christians can reduce their anxiety as they present practical solutions, plus the hope, stability and comfort in knowing Jesus as Lord. I expect increasing numbers of "preimpact salvations" to be birthed from the stark awareness of people's meager emotional and practical resources. Consequently, a newfound relationship with Jesus, "preimpact," will further mitigate their trauma during crisis, as well as reduce their incidence of post-traumatic stress disorder. Isn't that exciting? Oh, it makes me throb with purpose! Preimpact evangelism!

PHASE II—EVANGELISM IN THE PREPAREDNESS PHASE

Using the case study of Y2K hypothesized, let's continue. It's obvious that the closer we come to "impact" of any potential predictable disasters, apprehension builds and readiness activities accelerate. As we train others in preparedness, we can be salt and light among our trainees. We can explain wheat grinding and storage with how to purify water, while simultaneously building relationships and rapport. This provides a platform for evangelism opportunities.

Be sensitive! Your "trainee" may be hungry for the Bread of Life and thirsty for Living Water after hearing what you have to say about wheat and water storage! Be bold! I always say when evangelizing overseas, "If they go to hell with a full stomach and well hydrated, what good have I done for eternity?" Churches have a mammoth opportunity to demonstrate love to their community by offering formal, regular training classes like those of Pastor Bill Mendel, of Harbor Light Community Church in northern Michigan (see his story in chapter 13).

When nonbelievers are furnished with skills and knowledge, they will be grateful for your service and may inquire about your motives. *Your* peace and assurance will be an opening to introduce them to Jesus, the Prince of Peace! Discussions of alternative and improvised health solutions in calamity may provide opportunities to share about Jesus' healing power, and to pray for their current illnesses.

Competency for the task ahead is an absolute necessity! In 2 Corinthians 5:19, Paul indicates that we should be competent as a minister of reconciliation. In crisis preparation, we should give prominent attention to our soul's strength, stability and faith by *growing* in grace and faith, cultivating fruits of the Spirit and improving proficiency in moving in the gifts of the Spirit. It requires time and effort to fill our "Scripture Warehouse," but the Word gives life and will yield voluminous eternal dividends.

Our Disaster Training faculty advise much preparation, in both natural and spiritual areas. The following are pragmatic illustrations and exhorations from stellar leaders.

In July 1994, *Dr. Dora Akutteh* landed in Goma, Zaire, where hundreds of Rwandan refugees were dying daily of cholera. She advocates emphatically:

> The Body of Christ must believe our Commander in Chief in Matthew 24:7-14! I will constantly remind and teach *"Prepare! Prepare! Prepare!"* How? Train for disaster deployment at local church, neighborhood and professional levels. Study the Word and begin to apply it in every area of your life! Raise the foundations of strategic-level, serious intercessory prayer and fasting as the Spirit guides. I encourage every believer to watch the signs of the times carefully. *Make Jesus the Lord of every area of your practical life now!* If possible, do not deploy a spiritual babe into a disaster situation.

Dr. Khoo Heng Swee of Malaysia, who has led evangelism disaster teams since 1991, admonishes:

> We established a strong corporate prayer foundation with targeted intercession for the mission, team members and victims. We liberally utilize home-base and on-site

intercessors. Regarding raw materials (prior to calamitous occurrences), we purchase and collect medications, clothing, etc., labeling and storing, to hasten rapid deployment.

Dr. Joseph Paul Ozawa, a Ph.D. from Harvard, portrays the essence:

I have been a trauma psychologist for over 20 years, but the stories I heard and scenes of destruction in Indonesia recently were still very shocking to me. For example, on one stretch of highway from the international airport, a mob surrounded innocent victims, seized young females out of their cabs or autos and brutally gang-raped them on the highway.

Dr. Ozawa embarked from Singapore to Indonesia's turmoil in late summer of 1998. Severe riots in May left 1,200 dead. The violence was catalyzed by mass destruction of businesses due to a sudden financial collapse in which the currency value dropped by 80 percent! In one area hit by riots, 75 percent of the buildings were destroyed or damaged.

Dr. Ozawa ministered reconciliation between Muslims and Christians for 7,000 people attending one meeting. These people took his notes and videos and ministered in other cities to thousands more. *Before embarking, he trained 400 Indonesian counselors and physicians in trauma counseling.* He also organized safe-haven shelters and medical assistance, working through the Indonesian ambassador to Singapore.

What would Dr. Ozawa do differently? What advice would he give those who wish to assist in future crises? "I wish I could have prepared more in advance," he told us. "I had 10 days to prepare to go into this zone of destruction. My advice is, *Preparation, preparation, preparation!*"

PHASE III—EVANGELIZATION IN RESPONSE EFFORTS

Rev. Paul Tan, president of the Indonesian Relief Fund, reports from Jakarta:

> The economic crisis in combination with prior drought and pestilence which drastically reduced crop production, created severe food shortages and sky-high prices. Millions of poverty-stricken Indonesians were on the brink of starvation, no longer able to buy food, eating only one meal a day.

At this writing, 200,000 people in Jakarta and East Java have been fed by Rev. Tan's relief fund. He shared: "One of the people who received the free food gave this comment: 'How come you Christians are willing to give free food although you have been persecuted and hurt?' We talked with him, he received Christ in that place and now is faithfully attending our church." (Severe persecution of Christians had preceded these conditions. Churches had been burned to the ground, Christian schools attacked, and pastors' families had even been burned to death.)

An Indonesian Christian crisis evangelist relates: "In some places, we received threats from those who were afraid that we would 'Christianize' the people through the free food program, 'Lunch from the Lord.' The local (Muslim) government told the opposition, 'Very well, sir, if you do not allow these people to feed the hungry, could you feed those 300 people waiting over there?' As a result, the opposition let us open the distribution center."

Another writes: "We informed the local police about the free food to get their support. One said, 'Although the churches were burned and Christians suppressed, they gave free food!' So, we shared to them about the love of God and they came to our cell-group meetings and church service."

Dr. Alex Phillip, a physician who directs the New India Evangelistic Association, gives this gripping account:

In Adimali, India, September 1997, unprecedented rain continued for over three weeks. On that fateful night, a loud roar emanated from the mountain. A deafening blast shook the village at midnight, the mountain gave way and thousands of tons of mud came hurtling down, leaving behind 25 dead, hundreds homeless, and millions of rupees of crops destroyed. Electricity was gone— plunging the entire village into darkness.

Immediately we dispatched one of our workers to go to the site and bring us news of what was needed most. The regular road was blocked. A 12-member medical missionary team comprised of willing Bible College students, two doctors and Christian workers took medical supplies, food and clothing to this interior location. These precious people were still in shock and immense grief. Only two team members, Mrs. Jeanette Wilson, a nurse practitioner, and myself had previous disaster response training (through International Health Services Foundation). This was pivotal for our success. The rest of the team was really not prepared.

The first days were emotionally difficult. Just a gentle touch of comfort, an understanding embrace and our tears brought solace and peace to them. "I feel so much better. You were sent by God!" said a woman who had narrowly escaped death when her house collapsed. We sent several subsequent teams and saw many receive the Gospel. The church there has grown significantly.

Col. Ben Boyd, logistics officer with World Vision, epitomizes the message:

Hurricane Andrew cut its devastating swath through Dade County, Florida, which was reduced to a trail of rubble. The storm splintered houses, flattened cars, toppled trees, broke power lines, causing over $20 billion damage. Within hours we were on the ground, watching victims tearfully survey the damages. Federal aid was slow in coming. The Army ordered 14,000 federal troops to help. The main path of the storm was 20 miles wide, with winds up to 200 m.p.h. yielding tragic results: 58 deaths, 113,668 homes seriously damaged, 300,000 homeless, major power outages and sewer lines broken. Only $7.6 billion was granted by the U.S. government, while the total needed was $28 billion.

Pastors received many of the relief supplies. Those who had lost their churches wasted no time in setting up tents to care for the people and provide spiritual direction. They conducted frequent services and prayed for the people. The churches reported an increase in salvations. In addition, many salvations took place in a large tent set up in the impact zone by the Billy Graham Evangelistic Association. There were a total of 12 tent cities accommodating 36,000 people, complete with Porta Potties, hot and cold running water, entertainment for the children and places for worship!

A worker from International Health Services Foundation (IHSF) shared:

From January to December 1998, IHSF and its donors have been able to provide over 1,700,000 meals to a country (name withheld for security) whose appalling plight is famine. On visits to establish food distribution centers with monitoring, we were able to lavishly share good news in bad circumstances with government leaders. The Holy Spirit opened a tender, fervent opportunity to get on our knees, weeping at the feet of high government officials to do identificational repentance and pray for them. These customarily stoic, concretized, intimidating leaders were visibly shaken and responsive. (We exalt and magnify you, Lord!) Today as I sit penning this vignette for you, I again weep, aching for their dire situation, deplorable circumstances and dilemma of eternal dimensions!

PHASE IV—EVANGELIZING IN REHABILITATION

Dr. Khoo Heng Swee of Malaysia testifies of holding evangelistic healing crusades at night after counseling and daytime medical-dental clinics for a Thai-Burmese border refugee camp:

We had excellent results of salvation, healing and miracles. To God be the glory. Also in the early rehabilitation phase, the Karen refugees sat on the ground from 10 A.M. until 3 P.M. every day, praising, worshiping God and studying Scripture, because they had no other competing or distracting activities.

Col. Ben Boyd of World Vision describes the Mississippi flood of 1993:

It killed 26, caused an estimated $8 billion in damages covering 10 million acres of communities on rich farmland, with more than 200 counties declared federal disaster areas (all 99 counties of Iowa)! Extensive property and crop damage occurred, costing billions of dollars. Thousands of people were homeless in this seven-state region. The low casualty rate of the '93 flood was largely due to early warnings, evacuation plans and the protection of levees and dams. I was with World Vision, and we partnered with the Salvation Army, establishing our headquarters in a Presbyterian Church.

There were over 100 churches, synagogues and community groups formed to assist the people in the cleanup: mud, dead fish, algae and snakes of all kinds had to be disposed of. The church groups of all faiths and denominations did a tremendous job in organizing this. It was a perfect example of various Christian groups working together with a common purpose. People helping people: to see volunteers who came from all over the nation to assist the victims was a joy! Jesus Christ was the common denominator in our relationships. We were there for Him!

Here is an account from the International Health Services Foundation team of 42 professionals representing six nations:

When we ministered in Kazakstan shortly after the collapse of the former Soviet Union, the country was in social, political, economic shambles. We gave academic and spiritual sessions for 700 capital city professionals. Afterwards, we expressed regret and disappointment to the dean of the medical school because we had not been able to bring in $1.5 million worth of pharmaceuticals because the company had canceled its donation. To our shock the dean said, "What you brought was better—God!" Approximately 550 were born again, many healed and 119 were water baptized. To God be the glory! Indeed people come to Christ in crisis.

PHASE V—EVANGELISM IN THE RECONSTRUCTION PROCESS

Don Aaker, CEO of Wells of Life, provides these details:

Shortly after the Gulf War, March 1991, a unique opportunity was birthed from tragedy. Fleeing the wrath of Saddam Hussein, nearly 1 million Kurdish refugees were crowded on the Iraqi, Turkish and Iranian borders. A disaster was unfolding as 1,000 were dying daily of exposure and dysentery. Immediate challenges were logistical and practical: food, supplies to be transported to remote areas, clean water, sanitation, etc. Wells of Life International sent a team of engineers with construction workers to a makeshift, snowy mountain community of 130,000 desperate people. Excrement covered the ground—little privacy among the squalor. The first step was to protect the water source from animals and human fecal coli-form bacteria. Then, portable water tanks were constructed.

An extended period of reconstruction and development began. In dealing with physical needs and emotional scars, the Christian relief and development agencies took varied approaches. Some felt that giving food and helping physical needs (Matt. 25) was sufficient. Others felt the Lord had given an opportunity to meet physical needs, as well as sharing the "living hope" in Christ. Unfortunately, most well-meaning groups did not see spiritual fruit.

A number of these groups were so overwhelmed by the physical needs that they were consumed by it, and at the end of the day were left with no emotional or physical strength with which to share Christ. Others did not make sharing the good news of Christ a priority. After seven years in Iraq, I've seen how God uses disaster or discomfort to cause people to search for answers. During our time there, He gave us His love and passion for the lost, and we've seen fruit. If the Body of Christ is prepared and determined in times like these, it will see a great harvest.

Col. Ben Boyd of World Vision shares tender memoirs:

In late 1979, 5 million Cambodians were on the brink of mass starvation. Khmer Rouge had massacred nearly 3 million in a four-year reign of devastation. The Foreign Minister of Cambodia, Hun Sen, authorized World Vision to return to Cambodia to help in the recovery. Our most important project was to rebuild, re-equip and restaff the children's hospital. We were assigned six orphanages, each consisting of about 500 children whose parents had been executed by the Khmer Rouge.

We started a pig and poultry farm, a fishing industry and vocational schools, and assisted reopening of the medical school. We smuggled Bibles in along with the cargo supplies supporting our projects.

One day a woman asked, "Why did you elect to leave the comfort of America to come to help us?" In honestly replying, I decided, *If I lose my visa, I lose my visa, but I want to tell this woman my true feeling.* I replied, "We are here to help you because of our love for Jesus Christ, the living God who loves you and died for you."

Each morning our team assembled in my room for prayer. My communist government interpreter, Wanette, began to come during prayer time, but never commented about our daily prayer meetings. Eight months later I asked Wanette if she wanted to become a Christian. Much to my surprise and joy she said, "Yes." Just before I left Cambodia, the team prayed with Wanette as she was born into the kingdom of God!

PURPOSES AND TECHNIQUES

Weren't you stirred by these stories? The excitement of purpose in them is palpable! Have you ever wondered about your own purpose in life? Why were we left on earth after being born again? Why does God not just instantly take us to our mansion in heaven? Could it be He wants us to be salt and light?

AWARENESS OF NEED

Some theologians say that God lets us remain on earth after salvation to allow us more life experiences because He wants to teach us to rule and reign later with Him. Some say we remain on earth to become sanctified. But I believe that if the Holy Spirit can raise our "dead" human spirit instantly in the process of rebirth, He could certainly perform completed sanctification and a reigning character just as quickly.

Instead, I believe that our primary purpose for remaining here is, as our Pastor Ted Haggard teaches, *"To make it hard for people to go to hell from planet earth"!*

Misery and despair often bring pre-Christians to their awareness of need for a Savior! Furthermore, adversity often "hypertrophies" or enlarges believers' faith muscles. As Jesus declared concerning the prevalence of tragedies in the last days, the era for believers to fulfill their highest eternal destiny is now bursting upon the horizon! God's glory discharged through you and me in the midst of upheaval can bring more of His beloved children to Himself. How awesome to see a smile break across His face as we exude waves of His nature upon the shores of broken lives. That kind of "joy set before us" overshadows fear, panic and self-protection!

PRIMARY PURPOSE: SHARE SALVATION

If you're reading this book now, and realize that you do not have a personal relationship with Jesus Christ, let me encourage you to initiate that right now.

What do we mean by "personal relationship with Jesus"? All of us know who the governors of our respective states are, but very few of us know our governors personally, i.e., to call them at home or have coffee with them privately. That is an example of knowing about God and His Son Jesus, but not having established access to them by the divine protocol.

What is this procedure? First, we need to see the "disaster" of our condition without that relationship.

As it is written: "There is no one righteous, not even one; there is no one who understands, no one who seeks God . . . so that every mouth may be silenced and the whole world held accountable to God" (Rom. 3:10,19).

For the wages of sin is death, but the gift of God is eternal life in Christ Jesus our Lord (Rom. 6:23).

This righteousness from God comes through faith in Jesus Christ to all who believe. There is no difference, for all have sinned and fall short of the glory of God, and are justified freely by his grace through the redemption that came by Christ Jesus. God presented him as a sacrifice of atonement, through faith in his blood. He did this to demonstrate his justice, because in his forbearance he had left the sins committed beforehand unpunished (Rom. 3:22-25).

If we confess our sins, he is faithful and just and will forgive us our sins and purify us from all unrighteousness (1 John 1:9).

For it is by grace you have been saved, through faith— and this not from yourselves, it is the gift of God—not by works, so that no one can boast (Eph. 2:8,9).

That those who are called may receive the promised eternal inheritance—now that he has died as a ransom to set them free from the sins committed under the first covenant (Heb. 9:15).

But now he has appeared once for all at the end of the ages to do away with sin by the sacrifice of himself. Just as man is destined to die once, and after that to face judgment, so Christ was sacrificed once to take away the sins of many people; and he will appear a second time, not to bear sin, but to bring salvation to those who are waiting for him (Heb. 9:26-28).

But when the kindness and love of God our Savior appeared, he saved us, not because of righteous things we had done, but because of his mercy. He saved us through the washing of rebirth and renewal by the Holy Spirit, whom he poured out on us generously through Jesus Christ our Savior, so that, having been justified by his grace, we might become heirs having the hope of eternal life. This is a trustworthy saying. And I want you to stress these things, so that those who have trusted in God may be careful to devote themselves to doing what is good. These things are excellent and profitable for everyone (Titus 3:4-8).

In reply Jesus declared, "I tell you the truth, no one can see the kingdom of God unless he is born again." "How can a man be born when he is old?" Nicodemus asked. "Surely he cannot enter a second time into his mother's womb to be born!" Jesus answered, "I tell you the truth, no one can enter the kingdom of God unless he is born of water and the Spirit. Flesh gives birth to flesh, but the Spirit gives birth to spirit. You should not be surprised at my saying, 'You must be born again.' The wind blows wherever it pleases. You hear its sound, but you cannot tell where it comes from or where it is going. So it is with everyone born of the Spirit" (John 3:3-8).

After studying these Scriptures you can pray to Jesus, asking Him to forgive you for living for yourself and the sins you have committed. Then ask Him as Spirit to come into your life, forever reigning as Lord, Master, President of all your life's decisions and choices. This is because you were bought with a price—His sacrificial death—and you are now owned by Him (1 Cor. 6:20). Quickly find a life-giving church with buoyant, victorious, holy-living Christian friends to train you!

CELL-CHURCH GROUPS: MODELS OF EVANGELISM IN CRISIS

From the perspective of a missionary, I recommend the decentralized cell-group approach because it enables new Christians to flourish in a difficult climate that often necessitates rapid, radical structural improvisation. If there is widespread hardship, even overt persecution, a cell-church network is the most efficient organization for supply distribution, personal ministry and unobtrusive worship. Also, decentralizing distribution of staple goods is more manageable, and safer from theft and sabotage. The individual cells might at some point be required to function with less coordination and oversight than currently experienced in America, thereby relying in greater measure on each other's internal strength and resources.

We have learned so much from apostle Bob Weiner, author of *Firm Foundations Bible Studies*. His discipling style sizzles with the fire of God and Holy Spirit baptism (Luke 3:16). His methods are consistently and successfully reproducible. He has started thousands of churches in the last decade, both in the U.S. and overseas. We are especially impressed that he advocates people being born again, breaking generational curses, deliverance from evil spirits (if necessary), baptism in water and Spirit—*all within the first day or, at least, week of repentance!* He also advocates regular daily mentoring, with frequency tapering off in several weeks or as appropriate.

We missionary surgeons heartily endorse the effectiveness of this "bolus-dose," or loading dose, for new converts experiencing God. This approach rapidly achieves "high blood levels" of solidifying, stabilizing truth for newborn Christians. It is routine for new converts in persecuted lands to have their very lives threatened within 24 hours of becoming a believer, so this intensive-care or "high blood level of lordship" approach is an absolute necessity for them!

In contrast, do we in the West tolerate retarded spiritual growth because there are no real stressors to the process? We are taught to be tolerant and inoffensive, but does this mind-set cause delayed developmental spiritual maturity? The percentage of slow-growing baby Christians is so high that we diagnose the syndrome as "normal." If revival is anticipated, possibly erupting from the pain of mass misfortune, should we first check our spiritual genetics (DNA) to prevent replicating the "lukewarm gene"? The "slow-maturing" gene?

As an obstetrician, ordained minister and veteran of work in the 10/40 Window, I have concern for the "genetic weakness" that comes from inbreeding. Could the Church maximize our prerevival, "preconception" spiritual health for yielding Jesus' best born-again offspring? Should we analyze our current "Lordship species," then envision a stronger genetic strain? Perhaps that would require revamping our previously standardized discipling process.

Is our final goal in God's discipling process to see sheep or warriors? Depending on your answer, the process of training is very different. Drill sergeants and shepherds have very dissimilar styles. To persevere during arduous times, a drill sergeant's style of equipping saints is probably more effective for surviving, enduring, improvising and overcoming! But who welcomes the rigors of boot camp?

Scrutinize again Jesus' words in Matthew 24:9-14:

> "Then you will be handed over to be persecuted and put to death, and you will be hated by all nations because of me. At that time many will turn away from the faith and will betray and hate each other, and many false prophets will appear and deceive many people. Because of the increase of wickedness, the love of most will grow cold, but he who stands firm to the end will be saved. And this gospel of the kingdom will be preached in the whole world as a testimony to all nations, and then the end will come."

If these realities are looming upon our millennial horizon, do we need to call for "DDSs"—Discipling Drill Sergeants? In the approaching perilous days, I suspect that the spiritual genetics and maturation of new believers in the West will need to mimic more closely the process among new believers in Asia. Strenuous conditions require dosing with "spiritual steroids" to produce brisk growth of spiritual muscle mass as described in 1 Peter 1:6-9; James 1:2-4; Revelation 2:9-11, etc.

RESOURCE MATERIALS

We referred earlier in this chapter to *Firm Foundations Bible Studies* by Bob and Rose Weiner. This work on growing strong believers is excellent foundational material.

If you have not been exposed to the structural premise or how-to of cell-church prototypes, study Ralph W. Neighbour, Jr.'s "Bogota, Columbia Model," and *The Shepherd's Guidebook* (Outreach Ministries, Houston, Texas). Also see pastor Larry Stockstill's book, *The Cell Church in America* (Bethany World Prayer Center, 13855 Plank Rd., Baker, LA 70714).

As you recall the Incident Command organizational chart in chapter 4, doesn't it look very similar to the zones and districts in a cell-church flowchart? Could Incident Command design be superimposed on the cell-group structure and function, augmenting each other's purpose, function and productivity? Supply procurement, storage and distribution, communication and member monitoring, needs assessment, skills inventory, etc.—all seem much simpler at the cell level. I believe that merging these two schemes is pivotal for supremely manifesting the Church's mandate in crisis.

To grow believers within austere conditions it is critical to have quantity, quality ("meat" not just "milk") and immediate accessibility of discipling materials. These should be administered by leaders who run toward battles, not away from them (see Ps. 78:9). From our experience in Asia, anything less than that will not effectively conserve the forecasted sudden, net-breaking harvest and then reproduce the genetics of courageous, unflinching believers. These in turn will replicate stalwart, robust Christians.

UNIQUE OBSTACLES TO WITNESSING

Do you perceive that John Doe Christian is competent to witness to American New Agers or to Muslims, Hindus or Buddhists living within our borders? These people usually do not change their belief systems after flipping the pages of *The Four Spiritual Laws* booklet or being asked to quickly pray a "sinner's prayer." I raise the point because many Americans are now mesmerized by deceiving New Age notions—many of which are simply old Hinduism, from which Buddhism emerged. A discussion of crisis evangelism in the U.S. would be sorely incomplete without addressing the ineptness of most regular church-goers in confidently discussing karma and Scripture.

Also, Christians who want to minister in crisis, but who have never seen miracles, may find it difficult to minister to those who find themselves entrapped and tormented by demonic power. Antecedent study plus insightful, mature, faith-filled, consistent intercession are required to break this level of oppression from the principalities and powers (Eph. 6:12). For training in these aspects we highly recommend the books by Dr. C. Peter Wagner and Dutch Sheets on prayer; Cindy Jacobs's *Possessing the Gates of the Enemy;* George Otis, Jr.'s *Twilight Labyrinth;* with the *Spiritual Mapping Manual* and tapes by Doris Wagner on spiritual warfare and deliverance.

How to approach members of the Islamic faith is another major concern in outfitting current American believers for effective witness among traumatized people. Most homeland Christians are unaware of Muslim tenets or scriptural bridges to them. Further study is urgently needed in this area. Expounding on these issues is not in the scope of this book.

Finally, as indicated earlier by Don Aaker's report from "Phase V" evangelistic experience, we must address the assault on the faith of the caregivers who become overwhelmed by the enormity of human suffering in mass tragedy. Many rescue workers, Aaker reported, were so overpowered by the needs that they "were left with no emotional or physical strength with which to share Christ." This leads us to the next chapter, which will underscore the need for strong faith amid catastrophe.

Let's get busy! Let's strengthen our nets, fortify our walls and reproduce the genes found in believers described in the book of Acts (no chromosome anomalies, please!). Truly it's for God, and God alone!

FAITH AMID CATASTROPHE

BETSY NEUENSCHWANDER, M.D.

How can believers face daunting, dismal, morbidly terrifying, woeful situations and stand immovable in order to reach out to others? How can rescue evangelism workers avoid becoming part of the problem, as indicated in the previous chapter, devastated by a loss of faith amid the very disaster in which they are trying to be part of the answer? The purpose of this chapter is to practice "preventive medicine." Join us in applying "spiritual radiology," performing a CAT scan of the Body of Christ to detect any cysts in faith that might rupture amid catastrophes of biological terrorism, Y2K-induced utilities failures or even economic collapse.

Immersing ourselves in Scripture yields a record of saints who stood steadfast in the past, whose faith can inspire us when we find ourselves in the middle of critical dilemma. Put your feet up, lean back and expect extensive quotation of such texts in this chapter, because faith comes by hearing the Word!

Hebrews 11:32-40 is a passage that inspires and thrills me. It unveils how some of the great characters of the past conducted themselves under intense pressure:

And what more shall I say? I do not have time to tell about Gideon, Barak, Samson, Jephthah, David, Samuel and the prophets, who through faith conquered kingdoms, administered justice, and gained what was promised; who shut the mouths of lions, quenched the fury of the flames, and escaped the edge of the sword; whose weakness was turned to strength; and who became powerful in battle and routed foreign armies. Women received back their dead, raised to life again. Others were tortured and refused to be released, so that they might gain a better resurrection. Some faced jeers and flogging, while still others were chained and put in prison. They were stoned; they were sawed in two; they were put to death by the sword. They went about in sheepskins and goatskins, destitute, persecuted and mistreated—the world was not worthy of them. They wandered in deserts and mountains, and in caves and holes in the ground. These were all commended for their faith, yet none of them received what had been promised. God had planned something better for us so that only together with us would they be made perfect.

That exhilarates and emboldens me! These verses reflect the presence of faith amid catastrophe. Verse 35 really impacts me. Note the conditions—they were destitute, afflicted, tormented. Why was the world not worthy? Could it be that their level of commitment was so much higher that the world's "best" paled in contrast? How amazing that all of these witnesses were commended for their faith. They obtained a good report (I believe) at the throne of Jesus! Their example calls us to steadfastness.

CHOOSING BETWEEN FAITH AND FEAR

I have personally been in the presence of this kind of believer in Pakistan, Romania, Nepal, China and North India. I've seen this brand of faith fleshed out in the lives of believers in these countries. The Bible says a great cloud of witnesses is watching our choice between faith or fear in catastrophe. They set the example! How can we do any less? How do we follow them?

> Let us fix our eyes on Jesus, the author and perfecter of our faith, who for the joy set before him endured the cross, scorning its shame, and sat down at the right hand of the throne of God. Consider him who endured such opposition from sinful men, so that you will not grow weary and lose heart (Heb. 12:2,3).

We must look to Jesus, who *amid the "catastrophe"* of the Cross, became the Author and Finisher of our faith. Philippians 2:5-10 admonishes us to let this mind be in us which was in Christ Jesus, who emptied Himself, took on the form of a servant and became obedient unto death.

I think the essence of faith is making a decision minute by minute that Jesus is worth giving up our physical lives! When that decision is final, every fear atrophies in comparison. There is no other threat!

Observing the commitment level of our Christian friends in Asia, I began to investigate biblical aspects of maintaining faith amid persecution and suffering. In these regions, oppression and tyranny are still pervasive 2,000 years beyond the book of Acts! Christians there can say with Paul,

> We do not want you to be uninformed, brothers, about the hardships we suffered in the province of Asia. We were

under great pressure, far beyond our ability to endure, so that we despaired even of life. Indeed, in our hearts we felt the sentence of death. But this happened that we might not rely on ourselves but on God, who raises the dead. He has delivered us from such a deadly peril, and he will deliver us. On him we have set our hope that he will continue to deliver us, as you help us by your prayers. Then many will give thanks on our behalf for the gracious favor granted us in answer to the prayers of many (2 Cor. 1:8-11).

If these Asian Christians stood before us today, they would share the following verses so that we would be aware of hardships that require faith during crisis. Look at all these verses of persecution in the new and better covenant (New Testament):

You, however, know all about my teaching, my way of life, my purpose, faith, patience, love, endurance, persecutions, sufferings—what kinds of things happened to me in Antioch, Iconium and Lystra, the persecutions I endured. Yet the Lord rescued me from all of them. In fact, everyone who wants to live a godly life in Christ Jesus will be persecuted (2 Tim. 3:10-12).

That is why, for Christ's sake, I delight in weaknesses, in insults, in hardships, in persecutions, in difficulties. For when I am weak, then I am strong (2 Cor. 12:10).

To this very hour we go hungry and thirsty, we are in rags, we are brutally treated, we are homeless. We work hard with our own hands. When we are cursed, we bless·

when we are persecuted, we endure it; when we are slandered, we answer kindly. Up to this moment we have become the scum of the earth, the refuse of the world. I am not writing this to shame you, but to warn you, as my dear children (1 Cor. 4:11-14).

We are hard pressed on every side, but not crushed; perplexed, but not in despair; persecuted, but not abandoned; struck down, but not destroyed. We always carry around in our body the death of Jesus, so that the life of Jesus may also be revealed in our body. For we who are alive are always being given over to death for Jesus' sake, so that his life may be revealed in our mortal body. So then, death is at work in us, but life is at work in you. It is written: "I believed; therefore I have spoken." With that same spirit of faith we also believe and therefore speak, because we know that the one who raised the Lord Jesus from the dead will also raise us with Jesus and present us with you in his presence. All this is for your benefit, so that the grace that is reaching more and more people may cause thanksgiving to overflow to the glory of God (2 Cor. 4:8-15).

But whatever was to my profit I now consider loss for the sake of Christ. What is more, I consider everything a loss compared to the surpassing greatness of knowing Christ Jesus my Lord, for whose sake I have lost all things. I consider them rubbish, that I may gain Christ and be found in him, not having a righteousness of my own that comes from the law, but that which is through faith in Christ—the righteousness that comes from God and is

by faith. I want to know Christ and the power of his resurrection and the fellowship of sharing in his sufferings,
becoming like him in his death (Phil. 3:7-10).

If disasters come, man-made or natural, and allow us to
know and experience firsthand the greatness of the Lord, would
we be able to say that whatever was to our profit is now rubbish?
Again, let us gaze on Jesus:

Although he was a son, he learned obedience from what
he suffered (Heb. 5:8).

If we endure, we will also reign with him. If we disown
him, he will also disown us (2 Tim. 2:12).

Dear friends, do not be surprised at the painful trial you
are suffering, as though something strange were happening to you. But rejoice that you participate in the sufferings of Christ, so that you may be overjoyed when his
glory is revealed. If you are insulted because of the name of
Christ, you are blessed, for the Spirit of glory and of God
rests on you. If you suffer, it should not be as a murderer
or thief or any other kind of criminal, or even as a meddler.
However, if you suffer as a Christian, do not be ashamed,
but praise God that you bear that name (1 Pet. 4:12-16).

LEARNING FROM THE COMMITTED

Many believers I personally know in persecuted nations have, as
did Paul, a deep revelation of grace. I have wept bitterly while sitting at their feet and listening to them relive stories that highlighted for me 1 Peter 5:10: "And the God of all grace, who called

you to his eternal glory in Christ, after you have suffered a little while, will himself restore you and make you strong, firm and steadfast."

Grace is God's divine ability poured into someone, accompanied by an outward manifestation of its presence. Our Asian friends regularly experience not only great challenges, but such grace-filled realities as these . . .

May our Lord Jesus Christ himself and God our Father, who loved us and by his grace gave us eternal encouragement and good hope, encourage your hearts and strengthen you in every good deed and word (2 Thess. 2:16,17).

Do not be carried away by all kinds of strange teachings. It is good for our hearts to be strengthened by grace, not by ceremonial foods, which are of no value to those who eat them (Heb. 13:9).

As the days ahead unfold, sin will appear as a tidal wave breaking upon us, but we can "evacuate" with the company of the committed into the throne of grace:

The law was added so that the trespass might increase. But where sin increased, grace increased all the more, so that, just as sin reigned in death, so also grace might reign through righteousness to bring eternal life through Jesus Christ our Lord (Rom. 5:20,21).

Let us then approach the throne of grace with confidence, so that we may receive mercy and find grace to help us in our time of need (Heb. 4:16).

Indeed, even if our food and water supplies are exhausted and pharmaceuticals are expended, we can express our faith while surrounded by desolation because God said that His grace is sufficient for us, and His power is made perfect in weakness. Let's review:

Therefore I will boast all the more gladly about my weaknesses, so that Christ's power may rest on me. That is why, for Christ's sake, I delight in weaknesses, in insults, in hardships, in persecutions, in difficulties. For when I am weak, then I am strong (2 Cor. 12:9,10).

We can "prepare to share" material supplies, as well as faith, and believe that great grace will flow and blessings will be manifested to the traumatized! Set your faith—your believing, your relying—upon the following promise:

And God is able to make all grace abound to you, so that in all things at all times, having all that you need, you will abound in every good work . . . . Now he who supplies seed to the sower and bread for food will also supply and increase your store of seed and will enlarge the harvest of your righteousness. You will be made rich in every way so that you can be generous on every occasion, and through us your generosity will result in thanksgiving to God. This service that you perform is not only supplying the needs of God's people but is also overflowing in many expressions of thanks to God. Because of the service by which you have proved yourselves, men will praise God for the obedience that accompanies your confession of the gospel of Christ, and for your generosity in sharing with them and with everyone else. And in their prayers for you their hearts will go out to you, because of the surpassing grace God has given you. Thanks be to God for his indescribable gift! (2 Cor. 9:8,10-15).

Doesn't the promise of reward, fulfillment and throbbing purpose override all your fears? Apostle John Kelly makes my heart race when he preaches on faith. Having been in Military Special Forces, he teaches that in the military they do not need to make fearless soldiers, they just sculpt the training to produce courageous troops! When fearful battles and circumstances arise, courage overrides anxiety and fear!

Courage (faith) is not the absence of fear, but a tank that pushes past the roadblocks of paralyzing fear. "But my righteous one will live by faith. And if he shrinks back, I will not be pleased with him" (Heb. 10:38). Shrinking-back faith is not pleasing to God—a very sobering thought!

But Paul exhibited the "tank-like" qualities of courage as he wrote:

For when we came into Macedonia, this body of ours had no rest, but we were harassed at every turn—conflicts on the outside, fears within. But God, who comforts the downcast, comforted us by the coming of Titus (2 Cor. 7:5,6).

For God did not give us a spirit of timidity [*KJV*, "fear"], but a spirit of power, of love and of self-discipline (2 Tim. 1:7).

Notice that Paul said that God did not give us a spirit of fear. Yet Paul *did* experience "fears within," in Macedonia; but he pushed past those fears and walked in faith. That encourages me! In my friends from Asia I see a warrior's courage, as well as gentle submission to Jesus. It's amazing! They have very few conferences, tape series, books, commentaries—far fewer resources to facilitate faith than we have. Yet I am amazed as I watch them live out Paul's challenge: "Endure hardship with us like a good soldier of Christ Jesus. No one serving as a soldier gets involved in civilian affairs—he wants to please his commanding officer" (2 Tim. 2:3,4).

SOLDIERING IN GOD'S ARMY

David Shibley, one of our mentors, once told us that Rev. Peter Church said, "You can tell the whereabouts of a soldier by the nature of his complaints. The soldier, safe in his barracks, complains about the food, bunkmates, his sergeant. The soldier on the front lines has only *one* complaint . . . the *enemy.*

Where are you? Where is the "army of God"? As tragedies of the last days increase, fulfilling Jesus' prophecy, will we see a transition occur from barracks to front lines? As personal discomfort and inconveniences multiply in magnitude and frequency, the time is soon coming when we will be faced with crucial choices. Will the Church be like the men of Ephraim, who "though armed with bows, turned back on the day of battle" (Ps. 78:9)? Or will they run toward the battle, conquering kingdoms like the Old Testament heroes in that passage cited earlier from Hebrews 11?

Scripture proclaims that each of us has been given a measure of faith, that the just shall live by faith; and that faith is the substance of things hoped for, the evidence of things not seen. When there is a bull market, do we walk by sight or faith? When the American lifestyle is prosperous and very comfortable, do we make eternally consequential decisions by sight or by faith? If anthrax spores are released at the Denver airport, will we walk by sight or by faith? Why are Jesus' predictions of pestilences and plagues, famines and earthquakes, and the possibility of Y2K disruption being discussed in the Body of Christ so fearfully if we are truly grounded in faith, not sight? Are anxiety, fear, panic or denial diagnostic symptoms that our faith has not been proved genuine, as in 1 Peter 1:6,7?

> In this you greatly rejoice, though now for a little while you may have had to suffer grief in all kinds of trials. These have come so that your faith—of greater worth than gold, which perishes even though refined by fire—may be proved genuine and may result in praise, glory and honor when Jesus Christ is revealed.

If believers have clothed themselves adequately with faith, which comes by hearing and believing (practicing dependence on) the Word of God (see Rom. 10:9,10,17), then speculative discussions about prudent "preparing for sharing" in order to harvest souls should excite and challenge rather than provoke fear and protectionism! Indeed, the Western Church has not had the same "privileges" to develop persevering, mature, complete faith that is not lacking in anything (as described in James 1:3). Consequently, we might have a clinically higher probability for shipwrecked faith (see 1 Tim. 1:19).

To the Thessalonians Paul wrote that "Night and day we pray most earnestly that we may see you again and supply what is lacking in your faith" (1 Thess. 3:10). The key to answering Paul's prayer in the affirmative is *a personal, in-your-gut choice, made with resolve and gritted teeth.* It's a choice that affirms, *Jesus is*

Lord and Master of my life, all I have and all I can ever be. God of the Universe dying for me is worth my sacrifice and even death.

> They overcame him by the blood of the Lamb and by the word of their testimony; they did not love their lives so much as to shrink from death (Rev. 12:11).

We can make this kind of commitment because we're covenant partners with Jesus. He "cut covenant" with us, as the wording in the Old Testament implies, and in return we "cut and bleed" our fleshly desires and values, yielding all possessions, influence and family to our covenant Partner!

Over the last 12 years we have taken literally hundreds of affluent, prosperous, comfortable American Christians with us to India, China, Kazakstan and all over Asia. Sadly, we have watched many choose not to "fight the good fight of the faith" (1 Tim. 6:12) because of the risk, discomfort, hassles and vexation of living in a culture that deprived them of many "necessities." In future crisis scenarios in America, we ache to see members of the Body of Christ unanimously mix faith with the promises and character of God (see Heb. 3–4) to demonstrate overcoming victory!

KEYS TO STALWART FAITH

We offer here some keys that in our 25 years of experience have proved helpful for growing, then fortifying, faith.

- Meditate in God's Word daily and deliberately choose to trust in it (Rom. 10:17; Josh. 1:8-11).
- Regularly ask for much grace (2 Cor. 9:8).
- Stoke the fire of God (Luke 3:16; Rom. 12:11).
- Wrestle in prayer (Col. 4:12; Eph. 6:12; 2 Cor. 10:3-5).

- Believe that He is a rewarder of those who diligently seek Him (Heb. 11:6).
- Believe (the Greek means "rely upon") His promises (John 3:18; Luke 10:19).
- See Him who is invisible, through His Word and promises (Heb. 11:27).
- Fix your gaze on Jesus, the Author and Finisher of Faith, and resolutely throw aside every hindering weight (Heb. 12:1,2).
- Cry out, "Lord, let it be to me according to your word" (Luke 1:38).
- Continually choose to endure hardship as a good soldier (2 Tim. 2:3,4).
- Daily build your faith by praying in the Spirit (Jude 20).

When pandemonium surrounds us, the goal is to have great quantities of genuine, tested-by-fire faith in the "God of the impossible"! Then He is released to make all things possible for, to and through us as we stand upon our experiential knowledge of His nature, character and will.

The more faith we have, the more we can give away to destitute, suffering neighbors and our community. Out of faith will flow miracles, signs, wonders, answers, deliverances, aid, solutions, hope and blessings, all of which will result in thanksgiving to God.

The effect of a faith that overcomes is excitement. It produces the pulsating challenge and thrill of being able to shine brightly in darkness. If we stay strong in faith we become a beacon on a hill, vibrant with purpose and destiny, because:

Though the fig tree does not bud and there are no grapes on the vines, though the olive crop fails and the fields produce no food, though there are no sheep in the pen and no cattle in the stalls, yet I will rejoice in the Lord, I will be joyful in God my Savior. The Sovereign Lord is my strength; he makes my feet like the feet of a deer, he enables me to go on the heights (Hab. 3:17-19).

AVOIDING TRUE FAMINE: YOUR SCRIPTURE STOREHOUSE

MARK NEUENSCHWANDER, M.D.

The pretty young nurse stood before the TV news camera. Her hand held open the door to the refrigerator in her meager apartment in Russia. Pointing to three large jars of grayish matter and liquid, the only contents of the refrigerator, she explained, "This one is cucumbers, and those are mushrooms." Bitterly, she continued, "You want to see our savings? This is our savings." Her voice broke as she struggled to remain composed. "What will we do when winter comes?"

My heart aches for her and many more in the same situation. The cabinets in her home are empty. The fields have been harvested and there is not enough food left to store up for the brutal winter. She knows the future only too well.

AGAINST PANIC: GOD'S PLAN

In the days ahead, we are going to hear a lot of doom and gloom and depressing information; and if our Scripture Storehouse has empty shelves our hearts will be filled with fear.

During the Los Angeles earthquake in 1995, more people died from heart failure than from the actual quake. When people are terrified, they react irrationally. When sections of a stadium collapse at a sports arena, stampeding crowds sometimes crush more spectators to death than the falling bleachers. As we begin to go through the difficult times ahead, the tendency of many will be to panic and become overwhelmed with hysteria while they watch society crumble around them.

But stop right here! We can put a large canister of God's eternal, never-changing Scriptures on an easy-to-reach shelf in the pantry! Twenty large bags of God's promises can be stored on the floor. Boxes and boxes of faith scriptures need to go in the empty spaces. Let's fill the whole storehouse with bottles and bottles of living water and baskets of the bread of life! Then as we get God's Word stuffed into every part of our being, it will burst forth and feed us and others when the hunger pangs of doubt and fear strike. Our thoughts will be transformed by God's thoughts so we can bless those around us.

A FAMINE IN THE LAND

Famine is not a pretty sight. In August and December of 1997, we witnessed firsthand the effects of the extreme scarcity of food in North Korea. In the U.S., we turn away from these news stories and pictures of babies with protruding bellies, willing our minds to think of something else rather than take in the horror of the bony limbs and sunken eyes. "Thankfully, it only happens in other countries," we think, to soothe our minds. It is just too fearful to contemplate the possibility of ourselves or those we love literally starving to death.

But there is another kind of famine that is even more serious. God warns us through the prophet Amos: "The days are coming . . . when I will send a famine through the land—not a famine of food or a thirst for water, but a famine of hearing the words of the Lord" (Amos 8:11).

Has our own disinterest in spiritual matters caused God to send such a famine? Do we appear to Him spiritually as those physically starving people on television, with bony limbs, sunken eyes and protruding bellies, starved for His life-giving Word because we failed to hide it in our hearts?

Jesus rebuked the church at Laodicea:

You say, "I am rich; I have acquired wealth and do not need a thing." But you do not realize that you are wretched, pitiful, poor, blind and naked. I counsel you to buy from me gold refined in the fire, so you can become rich; and white clothes to wear, so you can cover your shameful nakedness; and salve to put on your eyes, so you can see (Rev. 3:17,18).

We have been in parts of the world where you cannot take a Bible. We were not allowed to take Bibles into Burma (now Myanmar) in 1989. It is even prohibited to bring a personal Bible into Saudi Arabia! On our trips into North Korea, we have had to be very careful. What if Bibles are ever confiscated in the U.S.? The only Bible people may see in the days ahead is the one you have on the inside. God wants us to stock our scriptural storehouse by memorizing enough scripture to keep ourselves alive, and to keep alive many people around us.

BE PREPARED TO SHARE
When people's hearts are paralyzed with fear, God wants us to save their lives by opening one of our bags of promises and sharing the

contents. If we have stocked our spiritual storehouse, we can share with them that "God is our refuge and our strength, an ever-present help in trouble. Therefore we will not fear, though the earth give way and the mountains fall into the heart of the sea, though its waters roar and foam and the mountains quake with their surging" (Ps. 46:1-3).

Prepare to be victorious despite circumstances by storing plenty of jars of encouragement! David had to encourage himself when his men were ready to stone him. He said, "I would have despaired unless I had believed that I would see the goodness of the Lord in the land of the living. Wait for the Lord; be strong, and let your heart take courage; yes, wait for the Lord" (Ps. 27:13,14, *NASB*). Disciplining yourself in the Word of God, the Bible, is preparation to be victorious despite circumstances.

Can you see the storeroom full, bursting at the seams? If you have built a reservoir of faith, you may have opportunities to see incredible miracles of multiplication in the days ahead. You may not have enough grain or water, but if you store provisions and are prepared to share this as the Lord leads, your faith in God can multiply it. People will be coming to you for grain, water and counsel because you will be a rock and a fortress.

Many Christians are asking, How in the world do I get the money for all this grain? How in the world do I get my community prepared? The answer is in Matthew 6:31-33:

> So do not worry, saying, "What shall we eat?" or "What shall we drink?" or "What shall we wear?" For the pagans run after all these things, and your heavenly Father knows that you need them. But seek first his kingdom and his righteousness, and all these things will be given to you as well.

As you seek to be a blessing to others and to establish His kingdom in their hearts, even in a crisis, He will be your Provider. As you diligently seek God, first for His plan and strategy and then to obey His leading, He will guide your preparation in practical ways. "Ants are creatures of little strength, yet they store up their food in the summer" (Prov. 30:25). God will show you in advance not only how to build your house, but also what to place in it. "Prepare your work outside, and make it ready for yourself in the field; afterwards, then, build your house" (24:27, *NASB*). "By wisdom a house is built, and by understanding it is established; and by knowledge the rooms are filled with all precious and pleasant riches" (24:3,4, *NASB*).

Hurting people will flood into your church because they are hungry, sick and diseased, frightened and seeking answers—people who otherwise would not darken a church door. The prepared Christian has God's sense of "accurate weights" or balance (see Prov. 11:1), knowing how to blend spiritual, emotional and material aid. He may take a little stored grain and prepare bread, some previously stocked medicine and ease the sickness. Then he reverently lifts the huge white box of redemption from his hidden reserves in the Scripture pantry, and freely gives the lost one what he has freely received. In large bold print on the side of the box is "JOHN 1:12—To all who received him, to those who believed in his name, he gave the right to become children of God."

THE CALL FOR COURAGE

God wants to raise up Ezras, who can rightly divide His Word, the Bible; Nehemiahs to rebuild the walls of our broken and demolished society; and Joshuas and Josephs to carry out His preemptive plans. Will you be one of them? God told Joshua, "I will give you every place where you set your foot, as I promised

Moses" (Josh. 1:3). As you begin to think about this, memorizing it, making it personal by visualizing it in your mind and vocalizing it, faith will rise up that God will make you a Joshua.

"No one will be able to stand up against you all the days of your life. As I was with Moses, so I will be with you; I will never leave you nor forsake you. Be strong and courageous, because you will lead these people to inherit the land . . . . Be strong and very courageous. Be careful to obey all the law my servant Moses gave you; do not turn from it to the right or to the left, that you may be successful wherever you go. Do not let this Book of the Law depart from your mouth; meditate on it day and night, so that you may be careful to do everything written in it. Then you will be prosperous and successful. Have I not commanded you? Be strong and courageous. Do not be terrified; do not be discouraged, for the Lord your God will be with you wherever you go" (Josh. 1:5-9).

Notice that three times God said, "Be strong and courageous." Remember that while God is no respecter of persons, He does commend and respect courage and faith. Joshua had to build his faith just as we do! When calamity comes, we will have to hang onto God's Word as never before. Do not turn from it to the right, or to the left. Do not let it depart from your mouth. Choose instead to diligently meditate on it! Faith will rise and you will be like the lion of the tribe of Judah, and nothing will be able to stop you. God will drop a Holy Spirit blueprint into your spirit to carry out His plan.

There is a sequence of events here. First, Joshua was to meditate on God's Word day and night. Then God told him to "Go

through the camp and tell the people, 'Get your supplies ready.'"
Next, God said, "Three days from now you will cross the Jordan
here to go in and take possession of the land the Lord your God is
giving you for your own" (Josh. 1:10,11). Get your home prepared
now with spiritual supplies, as well as natural supplies! Then God
may give you a plan to help your church and reach your city. If He
tells you to speak to the city council, or keep a divine appointment
to meet the mayor, you will be ready to follow His plan.

STANDING AGAINST SCOFFERS

Courage will be required to withstand the wicked counsel and
scoffing that are abroad in our land. God said, "Blessed is the
man who does not walk in the counsel of the wicked or stand in
the way of sinners or sit in the seat of mockers" (Ps. 1:1).

I was reared in a traditional church, and I knew a lot about
religion. I even went to a Christian college for a year. But, I was
not born again until I went to a fundamental, outreach-oriented
church during my senior year in medical school. The anointing
of the Holy Spirit was there and people were praying for me. God
shook my false, egocentric priorities, and I accepted Jesus as the
Lord of my life. Immediately, I was surrounded by a group of
students from Campus Crusade for Christ and Navigators.
These dedicated Christians helped launch me into the Christian
life with scripture memorization.

A couple of years later, while in my general surgical residency,
to my knowledge I was the only born-again Christian. I took a
strong stand for the Lord and witnessed to those around me. I
prayed discreetly in the operating room during surgeries. And
believe me, I was ridiculed! Some of my former classmates, colleagues and attending faculty laughed at me and mocked me. It
was so bad that I did not even want to eat lunch with them in the

doctors' hospital cafeteria. I would go instead to the patients' cafeteria to eat. Then, when I was not required to be in the hospital, I would go to my quarters, spend time in God's Word and pour my aching heart out to the Lord.

The Lord had blessed me with good marks from most of my surgical attending physicians because I worked hard and conscientiously. However, I lost my surgical residency because I took a stand for Jesus Christ. A thoracic surgeon constantly ridiculed the Bible during surgeries in which I assisting and operating. I said I believed in the lordship of Jesus and that His words were literally true. I then quoted Jesus' words about lukewarm Christians, from Revelation 3:15,16. The attending surgeon became so angry he threw the rib retractor across the room and left the operating arena!

However, when God took me out of that residency, He placed me in one of the top surgical residencies in the U.S. As you stand for the Lord, He will promote you. The Bible says such positioning comes not from human realms, not "from the east or the west or from the desert, But it is God who judges: He brings one down, he exalts another" (Ps. 75:6,7).

God also knows what is going to happen in America.

It is He [God] who changes the times and the epochs; He removes kings and establishes kings; He gives wisdom to wise men, and knowledge to men of understanding. It is He who reveals the profound and hidden things; He knows what is in the darkness, and the light dwells with Him (Dan. 2:21,22, *NASB*).

Only as our nation seeks to promote God and His priorities will He bless our land. Only if God is in our midst will we find eternal aid during times of crisis. If our faith and confidence is in the Dow Jones, or in mutual funds, we will be sadly disappointed, for only the God of Jacob is our true source of strength:

> There is a river whose streams make glad the city of God, the holy place where the Most High dwells. God is within her, she will not fall; God will help her at break of day. Nations are in uproar, kingdoms fall; he lifts his voice, the earth melts. The Lord Almighty is with us; the God of Jacob is our fortress . . . . "Be still, and know that I am God; I will be exalted among the nations, I will be exalted in the earth" (Ps. 46:4-7,10).

SOURCES OF DISASTER

Sometimes the devil brings desolation because he is a thief and a liar who comes to steal, kill and destroy (John 10:10). At other times, it is God who brings the distress. When Pharaoh continued to disobey God's command through Moses, it was God who sent the death angel—just as Pharaoh had caused thousands of innocent Hebrew boys to be killed during the time when Moses was born. You do reap what you sow. God does have His own ways of vindicating His people!

When calamities come, will we have forced God to judge our country for her sins? The Bible says that God's goodness brings people to repentance. Which is better—for God to shake up our priorities, getting rid of all our false foundations and allowing us to go through cleansing and purification, or for people to spend forever and ever in a lake of fire and burning brimstone?

Disaster may also stem from evil within the heart. Ananias and Sapphira were members in the early Jerusalem church, but they had sin in their lives from impure motives. They lied by pretending to donate to the church all the proceeds from the sale of a piece of property. When God judged them, "great fear seized the whole church and all who heard about these events" (Acts 5:11). God is going to put His fear back into the Christian Church. Paul says that the quality of our work will be tested by fire (see 1 Cor. 3:13). We will suffer as we are tried by fire, but we will also see people repenting, and miracles performed.

> The apostles performed many miraculous signs and wonders among the people. And all the believers used to meet together in Solomon's Colonnade. No one else dared join them, even though they were highly regarded by the people. Nevertheless, more and more men and women believed in the Lord and were added to their number. As a result, people brought the sick into the streets and laid them on beds and mats so that at least Peter's shadow might fall on some of them as he passed by. Crowds gathered also from the towns around Jerusalem, bringing their sick and those tormented by evil spirits, and all of them were healed (Acts 5:12-16).

Making Jesus Lord of every aspect of our life requires us daily to make tough choices. You will have to get involved with God's priorities. In John 15:7 Jesus says, "If you remain in me and my words remain in you, ask whatever you wish, and it will be given you." Immediately we think of creature comforts, of things we think we need ... a bigger house, a better car ... I want this and this and this. But James said we "ask with wrong motives" (Jas. 4:3). Begin to ask the Lord, "What are Your priorities for me and my loved ones? What are Your priorities for my church, and for my community?" As we choose to live for God and God alone, then our desires become His desires. We can say, "I have been crucified with Christ; and it is no longer I who live, but Christ lives in me; and the life which I now live in the flesh I live by faith in the Son of God, who loved me, and delivered Himself up for me" (Gal. 2:20, *NASB*).

FILLING YOUR SPIRITUAL STOREHOUSE

We will be no good to anyone without provisions of Scripture stored up to give out. How can we store up such spiritual resources?

THE POWER OF CHRISTIAN BIBLICAL MEDITATION

The psalmist describes the person who is truly blessed of God as one whose "delight is in the law of the Lord, and on his law he meditates day and night" (Ps. 1:2).

We began to realize the power of meditation while traveling in Nepal, and watching Buddhist monks chanting repeatedly. The Voice of the Martyrs organization in Bartlesville, Oklahoma, has been serving the persecuted Church by showing video clips of kidnapped children of Sudanese Christians. Taken from their families, their ankles put in shackles, they have been forced daily to spend hours memorizing the Koran. The enemy knows the power of meditation and memorization.

Meditating on Scripture is similar to a cow chewing a cud of grass. The cow eats the grass in the pasture, forming a cud in her mouth and swallowing it. Then later, back at the barn, she can bring it up again, chew on it some more, swallow it again and repeat the process indefinitely. Likewise, we can chew God's Word, let it go down into our being, then later, when we are working or exercising or relaxing, bring it up to chew on again!

Get a system for ingesting the Word, a plan to fill the shelves of your life with items for crisis evangelism.

For my own system of meditation, I picture the fingers of my hand. This reminds me, in logical order, of the five things necessary for meditation. Beginning with my thumb, I think about what I read. My forefinger reminds me to memorize. The next digit reminds me to personalize the passage. My ring finger tells me to visualize. Finally, my little finger says to vocalize the passage. I do not memorize the whole Bible, but I have memorized select, powerful, life-giving verses that have given me just the nourishment I needed in a particular crisis.

Thinking. The Bible instructs us to take every thought captive to the obedience of Jesus Christ. Paul exhorts us, "Do not conform any longer to the pattern of this world, but be transformed by the renewing of your mind. Then you will be able to test and approve what God's will is—his good, pleasing and perfect will" (Rom. 12:2).

Memorizing. Some people say, "Dr. Mark, I cannot memorize Scripture." Of course you can. Anyone can memorize. You do not have to memorize whole chapters, but you can memorize one or two verses a day. It takes only a few minutes, and those terrific promises will change your life! Use a strategy. Put them on the mirror while blow drying your hair, the microwave door as you heat food, the dashboard of your car, etc.

Personalizing and visualizing. In the early days of our ministry I believed that Dr. Betsy was the preacher and teacher in this family. She said, "No, honey, I think God wants you to preach, too." So I began to visualize myself preaching, despite the fact that, early on, I had an embarrassing stutter. I pictured multitudes of people coming to me for ministry. You can visualize yourself getting involved in ministry. You can have a personal vision of droves of people coming to you for comfort, compassion, hope, help, stability and practical how-to information.

Vocalizing. The Bible refers to the power of the spoken Word. "Faith comes from hearing, and hearing by the word of Christ" (Rom. 10:17, *NASB*). Say the Word aloud, so your brain has to listen and concentrate. By doing this, your thoughts are replaced by God's thoughts, and your finite limitations are replaced by God's sufficiency.

> "For My thoughts are not your thoughts, neither are your ways My ways," declares the LORD. "For as the heavens are higher than the earth, so are My ways higher than your ways, and My thoughts than your thoughts" (Isa. 55:8,9, *NASB*).

DAY-BY-DAY NOURISHMENT

Another practical system I have devised is meditating on one or more scriptures from a list of topics for each day of the week. In certain weeks I focus on 10 to 12 wonderful topics from Scripture that provide spiritual nourishment to keep me healthy and in the counsel of God.

Sundays: Salvation. On Sundays I rest and contemplate on verses having to do with salvation. I do that because the Bible says to be ready at any time to give a testimony of the hope that is within me (see 1 Pet. 3:15). My words do not draw people to Jesus, but He confirms His Word when I minister it under His anointing (see Mark 16:20). I have seen many, many people saved because I have made salvation scriptures a part of me.

Mondays: Faith. "Without faith it is impossible to please God, because anyone who comes to him must believe that he exists and that he rewards those who earnestly seek him" (Heb. 11:6).

It takes faith and courage to position oneself to be a blessing to others! Meditation can help make your faith so strong that you will "dare to be a Daniel" and do great exploits for God (see Dan. 11:32, *NASB*).

Tuesdays: Divine Healing. I have prescribed many pharmaceuticals and skillfully utilized the scalpel. Although I have loved the practice of surgery, even more exciting is to see God use the scalpel of His Word in some impossible situations both in this country and abroad. As Hebrews 4:12 says, "The word of God is living and active and sharper than any two-edged sword, and piercing as far as the division of soul and spirit, of both joints and marrow, and able to judge the thoughts and intentions of the heart" (*NASB*).

Since health care has been listed as one of the most vulnerable industries for the approaching Y2K computer problem, focusing on divine healing will be especially important. Also, at a national disaster preparedness seminar in San Diego in 1996 it was repeatedly stated that many of the Los Angeles hospitals are located on the earthquake fault line. We encourage you to meditate on divine healing scriptures now, as preventive medicine. Fill your heart and mind with therapeutic, curative promises that will bring words of life to you and others in the days ahead.

Wednesdays: God's Love and Forgiveness. If you are prepared to take care of several people in your home during a crisis, they may be sleeping on cots, on the floor or in close spaces. In such close quarters, people may become irritable and cranky, and hard feelings may arise. If you have stored up God's love and compassion in your heart and spirit, then His love and forgiveness will flow out of you even in cramped quarters! "Out of the overflow of the heart the mouth speaks" (Matt. 12:34). Put love and forgiveness in your bathroom cabinets. Then, if you must share water for a "military bath" (1.3 gallons a day), you can be pleasant and accommodating despite the inconvenience.

Thursdays: Protection and Finances. The more you realize that God and God alone is your "refuge and strength" (Ps. 46:1), the greater rock of stability you will be to those around you. Yet in a time of crisis it may also be necessary for the Church to help financially care for the poor, the widows, the disabled and single-parent families. A large storehouse for adequately and efficiently ministering to many people may be required. Perhaps current personal and group programs and expenditures should be reevaluated, and contingency priorities considered.

Fridays: Wisdom and Strength. Wisdom is knowing how to apply knowledge correctly, and strength is the ability to do so even in the face of opposition. As you pray, meditate and ask God for wisdom, you will be able to distinguish between God's plan and man's. "Many are the plans in a man's heart, but it is the Lord's purpose that prevails" (Prov. 19:21). We are living in the last days, in which knowledge is increasing more and more (see Dan. 12:4). God's strength in you will enable you to endure and overcome (see Isa. 40:28-30).

Saturdays: God's Peace and Anointing. God has promised to anoint us with His peace and His presence in times of difficulty. "Peace I leave with you; my peace I give you. I do not give to you as the world gives. Do not let your hearts be troubled and do not be afraid" (John 14:27). Further, He gives us power to carry out His plans. Psalm 92:10 states: "Thou hast exalted my horn like that of the wild ox; I have been anointed with fresh oil" (*NASB*).

While I am practicing this daily discipline I try to think about, memorize, personalize, visualize and vocalize one or two verses each day. As we spend time in God's presence in meditation, He is fellowshipping with us because we are abiding in His Word

Developing this habit will keep your spiritual batteries charged for whatever lies ahead!

Here is another hint. Whatever your areas of need, meditate on the opposite. If you are fearful, meditate on passages that encourage faith—over and over. Just as it is OK to have coffee and toast for breakfast almost daily, so it is OK to meditate on the same verses until the problem is overcome.

See appendix IV for the scriptures that have been most helpful to me in this discipline of meditation.

PREPARING FOR THE STORM

Before the storm hits, build your relationship with the Lord. "Seek the Lord while he may be found; call on him while he is near" (Isa. 55:6). Meditating on Scripture prepares your spirit like good food and exercise prepare your body. Before the storms of crisis and disaster strike, you must rid your soul of waste, like the kidneys cleanse the body of waste products and the lungs exhale carbon dioxide. Scripture memorization is like receiving a blood transfusion, only it will be a thought transfusion! You will energize yourself and visualize giving life, help and hope to others. Be sober, vigilant, wide awake and ready for opportunities.

WARMTH FOR THE WINTER

Snow five inches deep and a cold, damp Moscow winter was one occasion for just such an opportunity. During our seminar for professionals in Russia, more than 70 nurses from the prestigious Kremlin Nursing School attended. We had been teaching and ministering all day and were exhausted and spent when a mother who was a nursing professor brought to us her teenage boy, who was crippled with juvenile rheumatoid arthritis. Tired as we were, the previously meditated scripture came to our minds: "Silver and gold I do not have, but what I have I give you" (Acts 3:6).

Suddenly, the compassion of God welled up within us, and we began to weep with that child. Dr. Betsy laid her hands upon the boy and prayed aloud; then the power of God hit him. Suddenly he took off walking, then ultimately ran around the auditorium. Except for a touch from God, this horrible disease would render the boy a helpless cripple.

And believe me, revival broke out! A large group of nurses saw the miracle happen right before their eyes. The next day we ministered on salvation and healing in the packed-out "October Theatre." Our students, now graduates, prayed for hundreds of people, and the Lord supernaturally touched and healed many.

When you put God's Word in your storehouse, it becomes a powerful seed in the ground. You water it by prayer and meditation, and somehow it sprouts, leaves grow and fruit appears. It is a miracle! And miracles of healing, provision, wisdom and protection happen when you meditate on Scripture passages and they become a part of your everyday life.

As the rain and the snow come down from heaven, and do not return to it without watering the earth and making it bud and flourish, so that it yields seed for the sower and bread for the eater, so is my word that goes out from my mouth: It will not return to me empty, but will accomplish what I desire and achieve the purpose for which I sent it. You will go out in joy and be led forth in peace (Isa. 55:10-12).

Preparing for crisis evangelism by dwelling in the Word has also enabled us not to allow fear of traveling in disease-ridden areas, or being short on financing, to stop us when we are sensing God wants us to be there. We build ourselves up in our most holy faith, praying in the Holy Spirit (see Jude 20). We speak to demonic forces in the name of Jesus as we obey the Lord's command to go into all the world. Again and again we stand in reverence and wonder as pagan governments invite us in and God's light shines forth in deliverance, healing and disciple making!

THE SWEET AROMA OF GOD'S PRESENCE

In order to bring healing and deliverance to our country, the Word in our hearts must transform us—our values, our actions, our choices—then our nation! When you spend time reading and meditating in God's Word, you are absorbing the sweet smell of God's presence. The more you spend time with Him the more you will "look" like Him, and be able to share the aroma of salvation and practical answers to the people around you.

> But thanks be to God, who always leads us in triumphal procession in Christ and through us spreads everywhere the fragrance of the knowledge of him. For we are to God the aroma of Christ among those who are being saved and those who are perishing. To the one we are the smell of death; to the other, the fragrance of life (2 Cor. 2:14-16).

Have you ever been around a neighbor or coworker who is so carnal and sinful that just your presence causes him or her to turn away? You smell like death to them. The devils are aware of the presence and the power of God in you. But to those who want to be saved, we smell really good! We look appealing to them and they will be drawn to us because of our nearness to Jesus. His anointing "rubs off" on us!

The Spirit of the Lord is on me, because he has anointed me to preach good news to the poor. He has sent me to proclaim freedom for the prisoners and recovery of sight for the blind, to release the oppressed, to proclaim the year of the Lord's favor (Luke 4:18,19).

PREPARE TO SHARE, NOT TO WITHHOLD

Some people are preparing for the year 2000 and beyond in a panic mode. They believe there will be a catastrophe in one form or another, and they want to be able to escape to the mountains or some other safe place. Go, if God tells you to; but make sure it is God! The Bible says, "Cursed is the one who trusts in man, who depends on flesh for his strength" (Jer. 17:5). If you trust in your own strength and your own ability to survive, and run to a secluded site, you will be sadly disappointed. We will not reflect God's character if we buy thousands of pounds of grain and store massive provisions without being willing to share. Instead of prosperity, that will bring a curse.

> "Behold, this was the guilt of your sister Sodom: she and her daughters had arrogance, abundant food, and careless ease, but she did not help the poor and needy. Thus they were haughty and committed abominations before Me. Therefore I removed them when I saw it" (Ezek. 16:49,50, *NASB*).

Christians must not be the cause of struggles and fighting over supplies. We have to be very, very careful that God alone is our trust, not our stockpiles or our money.

> Blessed is the man who trusts in the Lord, whose confidence is in him. He will be like a tree planted by the water

that sends out its roots by the stream. It does not fear when heat comes; its leaves are always green. It has no worries in a year of drought and never fails to bear fruit (Jer. 17:7,8).

Dr. Paul Yonggi Cho of Seoul, Korea, pastor of the world's largest church, told us that during the Korean War in the 1950s, Seoul was overrun three times by North Korea. In the resulting food shortage, people resorted to eating leaves to survive. After the third occupation, there were no leaves left on any tree in the city. There was mass starvation. He said there were many demon-possessed people who had lost all hope in life. People needed physical and spiritual deliverance and words of encouragement that Dr. Cho was able to give.

During a crisis, God wants to use us like the leaves of the trees, always green, for the healing of the nations (see Rev. 22:2). Like oaks of righteousness, we will not be anxious in a year of drought because our roots are deep in the storehouse of God's Word. It will be a sharp, two-edged sword with which God will do incredible things through us. We will become beacons shining forth, to which people will be drawn like moths to light, and we can minister to them. Whether in easy or difficult times, we can bless those who are hurting and distressed as we meditate on His Word, allowing it to become an integral part of us by *thinking, memorizing, personalizing, visualizing* and *vocalizing*.

WHERE DO I GO FROM HERE?

1. Is God a "respecter of persons"? (Acts 10:34) Yes___No___
2. Is God a respecter of faith? (e.g. the Roman centurion, Matt. 8:8-13; Heb. 11:6) Yes___No___

3. Why was Joshua a suitable successor to Moses?

_____

_____

_____

4. What command of God to Joshua enabled him to be successful? (Josh. 1:6,7)

_____

_____

_____

5. What areas of your life (in your spiritual pantry) are most depleted at this time?

_____

_____

_____

6. What current strengths in your life does the Lord want to make even stronger to enable you to be a help and a blessing to others? (Please list five.)

_____

_____

_____

7. Remembering that it is by faith and patience that we inherit the promises of God, list the areas of greatest spiritual need in your life at this time, and place a scriptural solution across from it.

Need   _Scriptural Solution_

_____

_____

_____

8. What steps are you sensing that the Holy Spirit wants you to initiate to make scriptural meditation a more integral part of your life?

_____

_____

_____

PREPARE TO SHARE: MEETING PHYSICAL NEEDS

We are going to switch gears in this section to talk about ways you can prepare in a practical, physical sense for possible disruptions in different areas of life.

As we discuss these areas of preparedness, keep in mind that it is important to not only prepare for ourselves and our families; it is equally important to prepare with others in mind. Our slogan is going to be "Prepare to Share." Accordingly, some of the chapters to follow will deal with personal and family preparation, and others with preparing for larger groups.

This is not to say that you need to take responsibility for everyone's well-being. But it does mean that Christians have an opportunity to be of great help to many people in troubled times—if they are prepared. For instance, if you will take time now to learn how to make sourdough bread without a ready-made starter, and to bake it in the sun without electricity, just imagine how many people could benefit in a crisis situation because you can teach them what you have learned.

As we look at different aspects of physical preparedness, keep in mind that the subject is such a vast one that it is impossible to cover the subject in its entirety in a few short chapters. Because there are several books written on the subject, we will simply give an overview and encourage you to gather more information on the areas of specific interest. Two sources by James Talmage Stevens we have found to be most helpful are Making the Best of the Basics: A Family Preparedness Handbook *(Salt Lake City: Worldwide Publishers, 10th ed., 1997); and* Don't Get Caught with Your Pantry Down *(Austin: Historical Publications, 1998). Each volume has a wealth of information, as well as excellent source listings for equipment and supplies that you may wish to obtain. In addition, the Internet has many sites devoted to preparedness that are well worth investigating.*

So let's look at various areas in which we can prepare in order to be a better servant to those caught off guard by an unexpected turn of events.

PERSONAL AND FAMILY FOOD PREPARATION AND STORAGE

NANCY B. STROUD, HOME ECONOMIST

Many of us have experienced empty grocery shelves when an unexpected storm has been forecast by the weatherman. Perhaps we, along with our neighbors, have rushed to the store to stock up on food. It is only in recent days that our culture has become so dependent on the local market that few of us maintain the well-stocked pantry that our forefathers considered an essential part of their home.

Gone are the "good old days" of canning hundreds of quarts of produce, and of food cellars and other methods of food preservation. Routines such as these previously carried families through several months until crops were ready to harvest the following year.

Increasingly, we have become dependent on boxed, canned and frozen dinners. Our grocer has a fresh produce department where we can purchase the makings for a salad; that is, if we don't go through the nearest drive-in to purchase an already prepared salad, packaged in its own plastic serving plate. Our time spent in the kitchen has been shortened to zipping open a bag to microwave the contents.

Because we have fallen into the habit of stocking our pantry for only one or two weeks at a time, preparation for a crisis or even a long, hard winter will require a change of mind-set. Our assumption is that our favorite stores and restaurants will always have the things we want and need. In reality, our system of food and household goods distribution is very fragile. Re-creating the well-stocked pantry could help carry us through times when our normal food distribution system might be interrupted. Learning some simple skills in this area can help us help others survive as well.

FROM WELL-FED TO HUNGRY OVERNIGHT

How quickly can a well-fed population become a hungry one? A 1998 report from Dr. Alex Philip, an Indian physician from the village of Pazhampallichal, and an IHSF graduate, shows that it can happen overnight:

> For a casual visitor, this locale was the ideal picnic spot, with fruit trees adorning adjacent sides of the mountains, and a gentle stream flowing through the valley that was home to 2,000 villagers. On both sides of the village, the steep mountainous slopes were used to grow cash crops— coffee, tea, spices, cashew nuts, etc.—as the only source of income for the people. As unprecedented rain continued unabated for over three weeks, the water collected within the mass of mud comprising the mountain slopes. On that fateful night, the entire mountainside just came apart. A loud roar emanated from the mountain itself as hundreds and thousands of tons of mud came hurtling

down, leaving behind 25 dead, hundreds homeless, and millions of *rupees* of crops destroyed.

In Indonesia, the collapse came in the form of economic crisis combined with a drought which drastically reduced crop production, creating severe food shortages and resulting in thousands of hungry people. The price of food soared fivefold. This hardship was made worse because millions of Indonesians lost their jobs or suffered paycuts as a result of the economic crisis. Rev. Paul Tan of the Indonesian Relief Fund describes feeding over 170,000 in approximately three months, working through the churches in a continuing program to provide meals.

With these stories in mind, let's take a look at how we can prepare to be of service to those around us in times of crisis.

LONG-TERM STORAGE AND USE OF FOODS

Certainly the most logical approach to putting food away for an emergency situation is summed up in the phrase *Store what you eat, and eat what you store.* If we keep this in mind, it is easy to begin buying more items that we use regularly, and storing away the extra items. For instance, instead of the two cans of tuna that you need, bring home four cans and store the two extra cans in an emergency food pantry. Soon you can acquire a supply of food that your family is accustomed to eating without making a large one-time investment. Another approach is to buy food in bulk and store away a portion of it for a possible crisis in the future.

Several types of food are appropriate for long-term storage. As we introduce them here, each family will need to decide how much of which type to store. If you are unable to locate what you want locally, find sources by referring to the reference sections in the two books by James Talmage Stevens mentioned at the beginning of this section—*Making the Best of the Basics* and *Don't Get Caught with Your Pantry Down.*

CANNED GOODS

Storing and using purchased canned goods or those processed yourself has been a long-standing tradition in our daily food preparation for many years. By simply putting some of this aside, you can quickly start establishing a source of food for an emergency. The variety of canned goods is endless, but consider primarily fruits, vegetables, meat and fish for a basic pantry.

DEHYDRATED AND FREEZE-DRIED FOODS

Dehydrated and freeze-dried foods are a more recent way of preserving and storing foods. Easy to store and even easier to prepare, they are produced and distributed by companies that specialize in long-term food storage, and can be ordered for direct shipment.

This type of processed food comes in a wide variety, ranging from dried apples and diced carrots to tuna casserole and chili-macaroni. In this way, a family can essentially maintain their current pattern of eating without much adjustment. Although the cost of a one-year supply all at once might seem prohibitive to the average family, the cost per meal can be quite inexpensive. Look for vendors that have payment plans or staggered shipments if initial cash outlay is a concern.

MILITARY RATIONS

Military rations, or "MREs," are perhaps the quickest and easiest emergency food source. Readily available from wilderness stores and some sporting goods stores, they are an excellent way to establish a short-term emergency food supply. Many preparedness advisors suggest stocking a three-day to two-week supply of MREs for each member of the family, thus allowing time for an alternate food source to be established.

THE BASICS

The basics—namely grains, beans, nuts, seeds, dried milk products, etc.—are so-called because they have been the basic building blocks of good nutrition and daily food preparation for many years in every culture. Because these are low-moisture foods, they lend themselves to long-term storage quite naturally and are by far the best accepted and most widely used types of food. By buying some simple equipment such as a grain mill and learning a few new cooking techniques, the modern family can sustain itself for quite a long period with tasty, highly nutritious yet inexpensive food. The basics listed below are readily available in small and bulk quantities. Even though most families will have to learn new skills and new eating habits, the changes will be well worth the effort in the long run.

GETTING DOWN TO BASICS

Because the basics are so important, they are discussed here in depth, along with the how-to's of storage and cooking.

GRAINS

Up to 25 varieties of grains are available. However, wheat is the grain most widely used in our current diet, and it is the basis for most breads, rolls and pastries. Regrettably, modern processing removes the outer part of the wheat berry, thus stripping the wheat of many vitamins and other nutrients. The resulting flours keep longer and bake into lighter breads. Enriched with vitamins and minerals to provide better nutrition, these refined flours have become the standard way that we consume grains today. But just taste a piece of bread made from whole grain wheat. There is simply nothing more satisfying, tasty or nutritious.

While wheat is by far the most popular grain in our culture, consider stocking some of these other grains as well:

amaranth	oats
barley	quinoa
buckwheat	rice
white corn	rye
yellow corn	sorghum
popcorn	spelt
kumut	triticale
millet	

Most grains can be cooked as a rice or cereal or ground into flour for baking. Learning about different grains can be a fun family project that may develop new eating habits for the future. In fact, many nutritionists suggest incorporating these whole foods into your current diet before you actually eat them on a daily basis, so your body can become accustomed to the change gradually. And just think—integrating these whole grains and other whole foods into your everyday eating will substantially raise your level of nutrition and promote better long-term health.

If a person is allergic to wheat, consider substituting spelt and rye. Once wheat gained popularity, spelt (actually the grandmother of wheat) was forgotten and put on the back shelf. Used exactly like wheat products in cooking and baking, spelt has only recently regained popularity after many people developed allergic reactions to wheat.

BEANS

Beans are another important building block of good nutrition in many countries. The following list is an example of the many varieties available:

adzuki beans	mung beans
black beans	navy beans
black-eyed peas	peanuts
chickpeas (garbanzo beans)	pinto beans
kidney beans	soybeans
lentils	split peas
lima beans	white beans

A wonderful addition to any long-term food storage program, beans can be cooked whole, ground into flour or sprouted.

NUTS AND SEEDS

Because nuts and seeds have a higher fat content than either grains or beans, they will not store as long. However, they can add nice variety to a basic food program. Nuts and seeds include:

Nuts		*Seeds*
almonds	pistachios	alfalfa
black walnuts	peanuts	flax
brazil nuts	pecans	pumpkin
cashews		radish
English walnuts		sesame
filberts		sunflower

DAIRY PRODUCTS

Dairy products, primarily dried milk, are considered by many to be essential components of a basic food storage program. They can be used in food preparation and also made into yogurt and cheeses. Dried eggs, though technically not dairy products, are considered part of this group. Persons allergic to milk can substitute nut and seed milks.

SWEETENERS

In addition to sweetening for taste, sweeteners can be used as a cooking catalyst when making sourdoughs. Sweeteners include:

white sugar   maple syrup
brown sugar   molasses
corn syrup   sorghum
honey

SALT AND SPICES

Both salt and spices are important components of any pantry. They add flavor to otherwise bland food. Use spices to obtain variety in your meals when using the same basic ingredients. Also use spices to make basic grains and beans more palatable to friends and neighbors who may have different tastes than you do. Consider that in a crisis you might be sharing food with others, and may need to create different tastes by the judicious use of spices.

GARDEN SEEDS

Almost as important as any other item, garden seeds for vegetables and other foods can provide the means to grow many of the things your family can eat. Foods from a garden will greatly boost your nutritional intake by providing important vitamins and minerals, as well as adding variety. Remember to purchase open pollinated or nonhybrid seeds so you can save seeds from one growing season to the next. A reference book on seed saving can teach the necessary techniques that allow you to produce fresh produce for many years to come.

OTHER STAPLES

The well-stocked pantry will also have on hand such staples as baking powder, baking soda, yeast and oils to expand the variety of the dishes that can be created with the basics.

TIPS ON STORING FOODS

HOW MUCH TO STORE

Here are some guidelines to follow when figuring how much of the basics to store.

Food	1 Person/Month	Family of 4/Month
Wheat	20 pounds	80 pounds
Other Grain	20 pounds	80 pounds
Beans	10 pounds	40 pounds
Powdered Milk	20 pounds	80 pounds
Salt	1 pound	8 pounds
Oil	0.8 gallons	3.2 gallons

HOW TO STORE THE BASICS

As you acquire these food basics, they must be stored properly to insure their safekeeping. Rotate your supplies by incorporating some of them into your current diet and food preparation routines. This will provide an opportunity to experiment with new cooking techniques and new tastes before you are forced into a situation where you must use them for survival.

And while we are on the subject of storing food, let's review just why we are doing this. At a recent conference where we shared this information, I asked how many people had already started preparing. I was quite surprised at the number of hands that went up. Quite a few people have ventured out and started to acquire food for emergency situations. Most of these people are storing the basics. What a delight to see so many on the road to being prepared for uncertainties.

At the time of this conference, Hurricane Mitch had recently hit Central America and done catastrophic damage. So I also asked, "Of those of you who have started a food storage program, how many of you have sent some of your stored food to Central America to help those affected by the recent devastation?" I was shocked to see not one hand go up. *Not one!* How can this be? If, in the process of preparing our families for an uncertain future, we lose our sensitivity toward those in worse shape than we are, then we might as well stop all our preparations right now. If the only ones we are thinking of are ourselves, then we need to readjust our attitudes quickly. We must remember that:

> This is how we know what love is: Jesus Christ laid down his life for us. And we ought to lay down our lives for our brothers. If anyone has material possessions and sees his brother in need but has no pity on him, how can the love of God be in him? (1 John 3:16,17).

Although our initial motivation might be self-preservation, we need to quickly plant an attitude of servanthood into our hearts so that we will be able to demonstrate the love of Christ by sharing what we have with others. Keep in mind that when crisis comes, everyone will be in the same boat—those who have prepared and those who have not.

We must learn now to keep a loose hold on those things the Lord prompts us to store. And we must be ready to ask how best to use what we have when all are in need. How can we possibly store up enough to help everyone in need? That is not to be our concern so much as it is to obtain and store what we believe the Lord has put on our hearts. In time of great need, we may well be witnesses to the multiplication of the little that we have as we offer to share with those around us. Remember the following scriptures:

> I was young and now I am old, yet I have never seen the righteous forsaken or their children begging bread (Ps. 37:25).

> Look at the birds of the air; they do not sow or reap or store away in barns, and yet your heavenly Father feeds them. Are you not much more valuable than they? Who of you by worrying can add a single hour to his life? (Matt. 6:27).

FOOD STORAGE CONTAINERS

The storage container you use may well determine how long food will last. Most foods come to the market in paper or plastic bags and boxes that are meant only for easy transportation and temporary storage. For longer storage, it is recommended that you transfer the contents to food-grade plastic containers or metal cans with lids that will create an air-tight seal. This will insure that rodents and insects cannot invade the container. Further protection of the food from bugs and spoilage can be achieved by removing oxygen as outlined below.

Once a bucket or can of food is opened, be prepared with a lid to reseal it in order to protect the contents. "Gamma Seal" lids are the perfect solution to allow easy access to five- and six-gallon plastic pails. You can find sources for these lids in the books by James Talmage Stevens (see the resource list at the end of this chapter). Also, reusable lids are made for No. 10 cans. In either case, you will want to protect the contents of your containers from unwanted guests.

FOOD STORAGE METHODS

To increase the effectiveness of your food storage efforts, many experts suggest taking an additional step in the packing process—namely either removing oxygen from the container or treating the contents. This will kill any bugs that hatch after the container is sealed. Methods of removing oxygen include vacuum packing with plastic liners, adding carbon dioxide, nitrogen packing and using diatomaceous earth (DE). Refer to chapter 10 for details on each method.

HOW AND WHERE TO STORE CONTAINERS

Once you have acquired and packed food or water for long-term storage, be careful to follow these guidelines in storing the containers:

1. Store food away from gasoline and other fuels that emit an odor. Many containers, especially plastic, are porous enough to allow the odor through and affect the taste of the contents.
2. Do not put plastic containers directly on concrete, because they will absorb moisture.
3. Store containers in a place that is as cool, dark and dry

as possible for maximum shelf life. Ideal temperature range is 40 to 70 degrees Fahrenheit.

OTHER FOOD STORAGE AND PRESERVATION METHODS

Other methods used to preserve and store food include dehydrating, making meats into jerky, salting or brining and using root cellars. Any and all of these methods can be incorporated into your overall food storage plan to augment the staples kept on hand. Further information on any of these subjects can be found in your local library and county extension service, and on the internet.

HOW TO PREPARE THE BASICS

If you are not in the habit of cooking with the basics, here are a few tips. For further instructions, refer to Stevens's book, *Making the Best of the Basics* or one of the many cookbooks on the subject. As with any new skill, it would be a good idea to try out these new techniques before you find yourself in an emergency.

GRINDING GRAIN

You can transform the grains you store into breads, cereals and other edible foods by using a grain mill. The flavor and texture of foods made with these nutritious ingredients are sure to please.

A grain mill will facilitate the preparation of a variety of foods with grains and even beans. Grain mills range in price from $40 to $400, and are available with either steel or stone burrs. There are different schools of thought regarding which kind of grinder is best, but a little shopping should help determine the kind that fits your needs and your budget. Look for a grain grinder that can handle all kinds of grain, and can grind grain into different degrees of coarseness, including fine flour.

BEAN COOKERY

To cook dried beans, soak them overnight, drain them and cook them covered with water until tender (usually two to four hours). Most seasonings can be added any time while you cook, but be sure to wait until the beans are tender before you add salt. Otherwise the beans will have a tendency to remain tough.

NUT AND SEED MILKS

Grind nuts and add to pure water for a high-protein, tasty drink. These liquids can substitute for cow's milk for those who are allergic to dairy products.

SPROUTING

Grains, beans and seeds can all be sprouted. Sprouting changes them from a predominantly carbohydrate food to a protein food full of vitamins and minerals, greatly increasing the nutrition available from these basics. To sprout, soak the grains, seeds or beans for 12 to 24 hours, rinsing two to three times. Then drain and set aside to sprout. Rinse two or three times each day and drain. After a couple days of rinsing, you will begin to see sprouts.

Some products, such as chickpeas, will be ready to eat at this point. Other items, such as alfalfa seeds, need to grow a little longer. Check one of the many books on the subject or refer to the section on sprouting in *Making the Best of the Basics*. Adding sprouts to salads, soups, stir-fry and even breads will add a fresh taste, plus lots of nutrition.

HOW TO COOK WITHOUT POWER

Part of being personally prepared for disruptions involves planning what to do if your home is left without electricity and/or gas. If in fact power is lost, there are several alternate ways to cook.

PORTABLE CAMPING STOVES

Camping stoves can be used as long as you have fuel for them. If this is the equipment you plan to use, be sure to store extra fuel.

CAMPFIRE COOKING

Campfire cooking, also known as "dutch-oven cooking" is a great way to cook, especially in winter when there is a fire in the fireplace providing heat. To cook directly on a wood fire, use cast-iron equipment with lids and appropriate utensils to lift the pot in and out of the fire. Dutch-oven cooking is considered an art by many; so if this is a method you want to learn, it would be best to read about it from the experts. In brief, it involves burning a fire to get hot coals, then placing a cast-iron dutch oven in among the coals. In time, the food in the dutch oven will cook and create a delicious meal for all to enjoy.

SOLAR COOKING

Cooking with the help of the sun is a relatively new idea. It involves using a dark cooking pot, such as an enamel pot, in a box or panel that has been lined with aluminum foil or similar shiny substance. The principle is to capture the sun and focus it on a dark surface, which absorbs heat and thus cooks the contents. By placing a pot of beans in a simple, homemade solar cooker in the morning, you can have a fine, cooked meal waiting for you in the evening. Solar cooking has a variety of uses, including baking bread and boiling water. For more information on this most innovative subject contact Solar Cooking International, search the Internet on the topic "solar cooking," or read one of the books on the subject.

For information on wood-burning stoves for heating and cooking, see chapter 12.

RESOURCES

Back to Basics. Pleasantville, NY: Reader's Digest, 1992.

Getting Ready for Y2K, videocassette plus resource guide. Ken Klein Productions, Box 40922, Eugene, OR 97404. Tel. 1-800-888-1363.

Stevens, James Talmage. *Don't Get Caught with Your Pantry Down.* Austin: Historical Publications, 1988.

——.*Making the Best of the Basics,* 10th ed. Salt Lake City: Gold Leaf Press, 1977.

FOOD STORAGE AND DISTRIBUTION FOR LARGER GROUPS

MARK NEUENSCHWANDER, M.D.

In Genesis 41, Joseph, God's man of the hour, interprets Pharaoh's dream:

> Behold, seven years of great abundance are coming in all the land of Egypt; and after them seven years of famine will come, and all the abundance will be forgotten in the land of Egypt; and the famine will ravage the land . . . . Let Pharaoh take action (vv. 29,30,34, *NASB).*

The Lord wants to raise up present-day Josephs who know the signs of the times with knowledge about what to do (see 1 Chron. 12:32)—particularly in our day of increasing numbers of crises and disasters.

The preceding chapter focused on food storage for personal and family needs. In this chapter, although we will refer again to issues that apply to small numbers, we will expand our concern to include the needs of larger groups, such as the people you and your church might assist in times of crises. The information here will equip you to assess needs for long-term food supplies whether it be for one person, a family of four or a group of 100; and the principles here can be extrapolated to thousands of displaced people.

Throughout, remember the basic underlying principles of all food storage: *Store what you eat. Eat what you store. Use it or lose it!*

SIX BASIC FOOD TYPES AND HOW THEY BUILD ON EACH OTHER

Storing and distributing food for large numbers of people will be made more efficient if you will keep in mind the following six foundational categories. It is important to note the order in which these six food types are discussed, since each builds on the one that precedes it.

1. WATER

As chapter 10 will emphasize, water is second in importance only to the air we breathe. We can survive only about three days without water. Although we take for granted having water in abundance, in times of emergency it is heavy and bulky to store. Fortunately it is normally quite cheap to acquire before emergencies occur. (See chapter 10 for details of water storage.)

2. GRAINS, FLOURS AND BEANS

Home economist Nancy Stroud noted in the preceding chapter that wheat is the most widely grown and consumed grain in the world. One reason for this is that it can be processed in such a variety of forms. From flour to pastas to breads and other baked goods, wheat is used in many forms in various cultures around the world.

Wheat can exist in three forms: (1) Unprocessed, as in whole or cracked kernels of wheat berries; (2) more processed, as in bulgur, wheat germ, bran, rolled and flaked (similar to oatmeal); (3) highly processed, as in white flour, semolina and farina.

Wheat is also common in most cultures because it can be easily prepared and it is easy to store for long periods of time. It is nutritious, containing high amounts of protein, calcium, niacin, riboflavin and thiamin. Vitamins A and C are present in increased amounts in wheat that is sprouted.

The addition of wheat to water provides a quantum leap for nutrition and survivability. It is a versatile grain which, when kept properly, can be stored for 15 years or more. Even in Joseph's day the grain he gathered lasted nearly half that long, for he "collected all the food produced in those seven years of abundance in Egypt and stored it in the cities . . . huge quantities of grain, like the sand of the sea" (Gen. 41:48,49).

A grinder provides the ability to increase the utility of wheat. It can be used instead of potatoes and as a substitute for rice. It can make several kinds of breads. It can be sprouted as a substitute for green leafy vegetables. Dry wheat sprouts can be used for sugar. Cracked grain from a grinder can be used for cereals. Gluten from wheat can be made as a substitute for meat.

3. POWDERED MILK

Powdered milk expands the usefulness of water and wheat, as well as many other grains and flours. Emergency supplies should include powdered milk and dairy products such as yogurt. Whipped toppings and cottage cheese can be made, and, with a cheese press, hard cheeses as well. Powdered milk stores well for as long as 48 months.

4. SWEETENERS

Honey, the preferred sweetener, can be stored indefinitely. It is sweeter than sugar, and has a higher nutritive content and more healthful attributes. Honey is a catalyst in the preparation of some foods, since it is essential for chemical action in those foods. It is also a preservative for fruits and vegetables.

5. SEASONING AND LEAVENING

Salt, oil and leaveners are also catalysts, and essential to food preparation and body development. They are the least expensive category to store. Salt, which is critical for body cell functioning, stores indefinitely. Salt preserves meat and vegetables. Oil and yeast are essential to baking and for the chemical action in dough.

6. SPROUTS AND SEEDS

Sprouts and seeds are a good source of fresh, green, live whole foods any time of the year at minimal cost. They require very little storage space, and can easily be kept in quart size or larger glass jars. Equipment: quart size or larger glass jars, pieces of gauze, and rubber bands. Again, the famine in Egypt during the time of Joseph made the people aware of the value of seeds. The people came to Joseph and begged, "Give us seed so that we may live and not die, and that the land may not become desolate" (Gen. 47:19).

STORING LARGE QUANTITIES OF FOOD

Any long-term storage plan for large numbers of people must be based on staples such as wheat, corn, beans, salt and a variety of canned and dried foods, since these foods have an almost unlimited shelf life. If necessary you can survive for years on small daily amounts of these staples. In addition to water, an adequate storage program will include:

Ready-to-eat canned meats, fruits and vegetables
Canned juices, milk, soup (if powdered, store extra water)
Flour and corn meal
Sugar, salt, pepper and other seasonings
Vitamins
Ready-to-eat cereals and uncooked instant cereals (in metal containers)
Dry, crisp crackers (in metal containers)
Potatoes (fresh or dried flakes)
Comfort/stress foods—cookies, hard candy, sweetened cereals, instant coffee, tea bags, cocoa, chocolate bars, canned nuts
High energy foods—peanut butter, jelly, granola bars, trail mix
Vegetable oils
Dried spices (garlic, onion, oregano, chili powder, etc.)
Baking powder
Beans
Noncarbonated soft drinks
Bouillon products
Dry pasta

AMOUNTS TO STORE

Quantities will of course partly depend on environmental conditions and individual tastes and needs. We will not try to assign quantities to each of the foods in the list above, but the following can be used as a general guide.

Food	1 Person/Month	Family of 4/Month	100 People/Month
Wheat	20 pounds	80 pounds	2,000 pounds (1 ton)
Powdered milk	20 pounds	80 pounds	2,000 pounds
Corn	20 pounds	80 pounds	2,000 pounds
Salt (iodized)	1 pound	8 pounds	100 pounds
Beans	10 pounds	40 pounds	1,000 pounds
Vegetable oil	0.8 gallons	3.2 gallons	80 gallons

SUPPLEMENTING YOUR STOCKPILE

You can supplement the above staples with commercially packed air-dried or freeze-dried foods and supermarket goods. Rice, popcorn and varieties of beans are nutritious and long lasting.

Part of our purpose in writing this book is to encourage you to build up a stockpile of easily stored foods long before a crisis occurs, so you will be ready to care for your family and for others at a moment's notice. Store up your everyday stock of canned goods until you have a two-week to one-month surplus. Rotate it periodically to maintain a supply of common foods that will not require special preparation, water or cooking. Freeze-dried or air-dried meats, although costly, will be your best form of meat to store, so buy accordingly.

GUIDELINES FOR STORING FOODS

1. Select the highest quality storage-grade foods possible.
2. Store only what you and other people will normally eat! This will greatly eliminate food spoilage, minimize food deterioration and stabilize diets during stressful situations, while providing insurance against malnutrition. *Remember that when people are frightened, upset and insecure, familiar foods can be a source of security.*

3. When possible, have people—at least your family—eat from stored supplies on a regular basis to accustom their taste buds to these items. This will also help in rotating the food.

4. Be sure to rotate items with a shorter shelf life in storage. Follow the "first in/first out" rule: the first foods to go into storage are the first to be used.

5. Foods must be clean at the time they are purchased and when packaged, and must be placed in clean containers free of insects. The containers must be sealed to keep out insects, pests and moisture.

6. The rates at which foods deteriorate depend upon the particular food, its purity, the way in which it is stored and especially on the environmental temperature.

7. Locate food storage in a dry, cool place, below 70 degrees fahrenheit. Foods should be stored as close to 40 degrees fahrenheit as possible. The warmer the ambient air, the more rapidly the food will become rancid. For every 20-degree increase in storage temperature, the shelf life of stored food is decreased by almost half. Remember also that moisture hardens and spoils all forms of stored foods. A damp storage place will crystallize or harden foods such as sugars, powdered products (such as flour and baking powder), processed foods (such as cereals), canned or glass-contained vegetables, meats, soups and or fish. (In contrast, the air in Egypt's pyramids was so dry that edible and sproutable wheat was discovered in them after centuries of storage!)

8. Foods that have their natural structure broken up, such as cracked wheat and flour from whole wheat and corn, polished rice, etc., may become rancid when stored unsealed.

9. Many dried vegetables, including corn, green beans and green peas, can become rancid when kept in unsealed containers.

NOTES ON PACKAGING

GLASS CONTAINERS

Glass containers can pose difficulties in some situations. In addition to being subject to breaking, glass is heavy, does not stack well, lets in light and can be quite expensive. If glass containers are used, they must be stored in a dark location. On the other hand, some fruits, such as tomatoes, apples, oranges and pineapples, will keep longer in glass containers than in metal due to their high acidity. All glass containers should have airtight seals.

The cost of glass containers can be lowered by saving glass bottles from salad dressings, pickles and other purchased items. The smaller jars can be used for fruits and vegetables, while gallon jugs and jars are suitable for storing rice, beans, powdered milk, etc.

PLASTIC CONTAINERS

Rigid, round plastic containers protect contents better than square ones. Bulk-packaged foods, especially flour, granulated sugar and powdered milk, should be immediately repacked in clean and dry metal, glass or plastic containers, then sealed with airtight lids.

Be sure that all containers are rodent proof. Small, round plastic buckets can be chewed through by rats, but mice will not generally attack plastic buckets.

METAL CONTAINERS

Food-grade, heavy-duty, sealable plastic liners in new galvanized drums provide good storage, and are rodent- and insect-proof if they are in good condition and tightly sealed. On the other hand, metal containers often rust through and spoil food. Prevention is best achieved by keeping storage containers away from moisture-inducing surfaces such as concrete floors. Place cardboard, plywood or pieces of lumber beneath metal cans to prevent direct contact with dirt or concrete.

STORING FOOD SAFELY

ELIMINATING MOISTURE AND MOLD

Moldy foods must always be discarded. Mold can grow even in a very low-moisture environment and is the primary cause of spoilage in stored foods. Mold spores are abundant in the air and can live on almost any type of food. They produce the most poisonous toxins known, and in seeds, cereals and nuts can cause permanent damage to internal organs. Moisture is excluded only by maintaining an airtight seal. Be sure that all containers are rodent proof.

INSECT AND RODENT PROBLEMS

When insects are packaged in food products they can multiply easily. Although foods such as wheat and other grains can be treated for many insects, if there is evidence of larger pests such as mice or rats, the food must be discarded. On the other hand, weevils found in stored grains and some processed grain products such as flour do not contaminate the product and the material is edible without harm to humans.

In wheat, insects are eliminated by using dry ice, freezing, heating and organic methods. Dry ice eliminates pests that require oxygen by replacing the atmosphere in the container with carbon dioxide. This gas, released from evaporating dry ice, will kill all animal life in the container, without harming the foodstuff.

There are two methods of treating food in this way. In one, a quarter pound of dry ice is placed in the top of an almost-full five-gallon container on an insulating material such as paper. Press the lid down gently so some air can escape. Wait for 20 to 30 minutes until the ice has evaporated, then remove the material and close the container.

The other method is to place the dry ice on the bottom of the container, wait for 20 to 30 minutes and close the lid loosely. If the container does not bulge, then close completely.

Heating and freezing will also kill any bugs in the container. In the heating method, place one-half inch of the infested food in a shallow baking pan, and bake in a preheated 150-degree oven for 15 to 20 minutes. Two precautions are: over-heating can kill wheat; and the freezing method may not kill all insect eggs unless the material is refrozen after 30 days.

The organic method of killing insects requires diatomaceous earth—highly porous and crumbly material that also eliminates oxygen but is not harmful to humans. In treating grain, one and one-fourth cups of the material is placed in the container, which is then shaken or rolled vigorously until all the grains are dusted. The grain is rinsed before using and blotted dry with a towel to wipe off the powder. This method works best with whole grains, beans, dried foods and processed grains such as rolled oats and cereals.

GUIDELINES FOR BUYING AND STORING WHEAT

1. Buy a variety of the best grades available, grain that has been cleaned for human consumption and is free from all foreign matter. Varieties to buy include dark hard

winter, spring wheat, dark turkey red, and Montana white wheat because they store best.

2. Buy wheat with at least 13 percent protein content, preferably higher. One source advertises wheat with protein in excess of 18 percent (Wheat Montana Farms, Box 647, Three Forks, MT 59752; tel. 1-800-535-2798).

3. The moisture content of the grain should not exceed 10 percent.

4. Use crush-proof, waterproof and moisture-proof containers.

5. It is preferable to store wheat in round containers so air can circulate around them. When using square containers, allow several inches of open space on all sides of the cans to allow the air to circulate more freely.

6. The best containers for storing bulk whole wheat are round, five-gallon metal buckets with enamel-coated interiors, airtight lids and waterproof seals. These buckets will hold approximately 35 pounds of wheat, which makes them convenient for transporting, long-term storage and easy use. These buckets will stack safely, allow better ventilation, protect the contents and require less storage space than barrels.

7. Round, five-gallon plastic buckets with tight-fitting lids and waterproof seals are a good alternative to metal buckets or cans.

8. Use heavy duty, food-grade, sealable, plastic liners in any containers for bulk wheat. The plastic liner prevents infiltration of contaminants, infestation and moisture.

9. Do not store wheat in containers that hold more than two bushels of wheat, or 100 pounds. Large containers are difficult to move and any infiltration, infestation,

spoilage or exposure will contaminate more wheat.

10. Store in a cool, dry place. Do not store near hot or cold water pipes, heating ducts, steam pipes, washing machines, clothes dryers or where laundry is hung to dry. Do not store in an unheated garage or noninsulated space. Do not put salt in stored wheat.

11. If you store wheat in bulk, you must have access to a wheat grinder. In addition to the more expensive electric grinders available, you can purchase grinders that are hand-, foot-, or bicycle-operated. The more a wheat grinder is used, the better it grinds the wheat into flour.

12. The shelf life of flour is very short at best. Keep all types of fresh-ground (store-bought) flours in a refrigerator or in a cool, dry place. Refrigeration at 40 degrees fahrenheit will extend shelf life of ground wheat approximately six months. Therefore grind only enough wheat for use within one week.

GENERAL STORAGE GUIDELINES

SHELF LIFE

The importance of selecting cool, dry storage space is illustrated by the following examples of the storage life of canned fruits and vegetables in Colorado, where humidity is usually not a problem.

Canned Fruits	*Shelf Life*
applesauce, fruit salad, pears, pineapples	36 mos.
grapefruit, peaches	36+ mos.

Canned Vegetables	*Shelf Life*
beans, corn, hominy, peas, carrots	96 mos.
potatoes (sweet & white), squash, tomatoes, pumpkin	48+ mos.

CHECKLIST FOR OPEN STORAGE

- Select a location on high ground with good drainage.
- Use pallets or wood to keep the commodities at least 10 cm. or four to six inches off the ground.
- Protect the sides and top of the commodity and lash down securely.
- Dig run-off ditches around the stacks.
- Secure the area, fencing it if possible.
- Establish fire-prevention measures.

CHECKLIST FOR COVERED STORAGE

- The warehouse should be near the main road so large-capacity, long-haul trucks can service them.
- Keep the warehouse clean at all times.
- Restrict the warehouse to authorized personnel.
- Beware of insect and rodent infestation, and if signs appear take quick action to control them.
- Stack commodities by separate lots, and use the general rule of "first in first out" for all incoming and outgoing commodities.
- Leave between one and two yards or meters between stacks and walls for good ventilation and fire prevention.
- Bags should ideally be between 55 pounds (25 kg.) and 110 pounds (50 kg.).
- Try not to stack items more than six feet (two meters) high, to facilitate handling.
- The warehouse should be dry, well ventilated and waterproof.

- The storage facility should have spare capacity to accommodate more supplies in case of unexpected or extended demand for relief.
- Do not store flammable items in the same warehouse as relief supplies.

MEASUREMENT EQUIVALENTS

Since many suppliers use the metric system in shipping large lots, you should learn the basic terminology and equivalents.

1 short ton = 2,000 lbs.

1 long ton (Great Britain) = 2,240 lbs.

1 freight ton = 20 bushels of wheat

1 shipping ton at sea = 40 cubic feet

1 meter = 1.1 yds. = 3.28 ft.

1 metric ton requires 2 cubic meters or approx. 6 cu. ft. (length, width and height)

SAMPLE SPACE REQUIREMENTS

1 Metric Ton	Space Required
Grain	2 cubic meters (6 x 6 x 6 ft.)
Medical supplies	3 cubic meters (9 x 9 x 9 ft.)
Blankets (about 700, compressed)	4 to 5 cubic meters
Blankets (loose)	9 cubic meters

WHERE DO YOU GO FROM HERE?

With the foregoing facts and figures in mind, here is a checklist for you to use to plan your strategy as you prepare for an emergency or disaster.

1. For what duration do you anticipate needing to store food?

   2 wks.___ 2 mos.___ 6 mos.___ 1 yr.___ 2 yrs.___ 5 yrs.___ other___

2. Have you made plans to purchase a grain grinder for you and your family?

3. How many people are you or your group preparing to store food for?

   2___ 4___ 20___ 100___ 1000___ more___

4. What do you have to offer (time, a strong back, computer and logistical skills, storage space, money, etc.) that would be of benefit in facilitating the storage of food and other emergency supplies?

   _____

   _____

   _____

5. Compose a list of essential food items that you and your group would and could eat from the foundation categories and long-term food storage staples (see p. 4), and add foods of your choice to the list. Allow for as much variety as possible.

Food	1 Person/Month	Family of 4/Month	100 People/Month
Wheat	__ pounds	__ pounds	__ pounds
Powd. milk	__ pounds	__ pounds	__ pounds
Corn	__ pounds	__ pounds	__ pounds
Salt (iodized)	__ pound	__ pounds	__ pounds
Beans	__ pounds	__ pounds	__ pounds
Vegetable oil	__ gallons	__ gallons	__ gallons

6. Where in your home, your church or your community would be the most suitable place (providing enough well-lit space and a cool, dry environment) to store food items for long-term use?

7. Are there granaries, farmer co-ops and grocery chains from which you or your   group might purchase items by the case lot to reduce costs?

RESOURCES

Boyd, Col. Ben. *Getting It There: A Logistics Handbook for Relief and Development.* Monrovia, Calif.: World Vision International/MARC Publishers, 1987.

Davis, Ian and Michael Wall. "Management Capsules: Practical Matters." *Christian Perspectives on Disaster Management,* 1992.

Federal Emergency Management Agency (FEMA). *Long-Term Food Supplies and Ways to Supplement Your Long-Term Stockpile.* Available from http://fema.com; INTERNET.

Handbook for Emergencies. Part One: Field Operations. Geneva, Switzerland: The United Nations High Commission for Refugees, 1982.

High, David. *Y2K Preparedness Booklet.* Oklahoma City: Millennial Technologies, 1998. Tel. 405-478-4351.

O'Riley, Paloma. *Individual and Community Preparation for Y2K.* Louisville, CO: The Cassandra Project. Available from http://millennia-bcs.com/casframe.htm; INTERNET.

Stevens, James Talmage. *Making the Best of the Basics.* 10th ed. Salt Lake City: Gold Leaf Press, 1997.

Zabriskie, Bob R. *Family Storage Plan.* Salt Lake City: Bookcraft Publishers, n.d. A compilation of suggestions for the preparation, preservation and storage of foods.

WATER AND SANITATION

MARK NEUENSCHWANDER, M.D.

Water is by far the most important practical or physical issue in preparing for an uncertain future. It is possible to live for weeks without food, but humans survive only a few days without water.

We take for granted the fact that most people currently have ready access to clean, drinkable water any time we want it. But what can happen if that wonderful system is disrupted? Let's look at some examples of what has happened in different parts of the world when disaster has struck to see if we can begin to grasp how important it is to be able to obtain clean, drinkable water.

WATER, WATER EVERYWHERE, AND NOT A DROP TO DRINK

DISEASE IN ZAIRE

Dr. Dora Akuetteh, a physician returning from a camp of 450,000 displaced people in Goma, Zaire, reported in our first Disaster Response Training School in 1995 that "People were defecating in the creeks and then drinking downstream, so without proper sanitation they were dying within hours. The immediate problem was cholera, a severe form of gastroenteritis caused by a bacteria transmitted from person to person."

"Think about it," civil engineer Heidi Falk-Gill reflected, "In Goma, when we were looking at 450,000 people needing a minimum of 10 gallons of water per person per day, that's 4.5 million gallons of water for bare necessities! It is amazing to try to get a handle on this type of situation. All we are talking about is sanitation, hygiene and drinking water."

The International Health Services Foundation was called on to help supply more than 30 people to assist Operation Blessing's efforts to help refugees fleeing to refugee camps. At an IHSF roundtable discussion in 1995, Foundation workers reported that:

> The underlying social and demanding physical problems, and the ultimate problem of disease, was that in Burundi and Rwanda, in South Central Africa, the Tutsi and Hutu tribes were killing each other and throwing the dead bodies into Lake Victoria, which polluted the water supply for three countries during the crisis in Zaire. Many, many people who were not even victims of the Rwanda situation died because of the tainted water. Within 24 to 36 hours, there were 300,000 people displaced, and ultimately it became hundreds and thousands more people who were basically stranded on lava rock. It is not normally possible to dig a latrine in lava rock.

AMONG FLEEING KURDS

Don Aaker of Wells for Life arrived by helicopter on the border between Iraq, Turkey and Iran when nearly a million Kurdish refugees were fleeing the wrath of Saddam Hussein. He reports:

A humanitarian disaster was dramatically unfolding as nearly 1,000 men, women and children were dying daily of exposure and dysentery. Excrement covered the area because it was difficult to find a place of privacy amid the squalor. Poor quality plastic pipe had been run from unprotected springs in the surrounding hillsides. In some places the broken plastic pipe had been routed adjacent to outhouses which further down supplied drinking water—polluted drinking water.

IT CAN HAPPEN HERE, TOO

Closer to home, consider this: during Hurricane Andrew in Florida, bottled water was brought in by truck and sold at outrageously high prices to the victims. People can go several days without food if necessary, but they can survive only three days without water. Thus, in a crisis, the single most important item to consider is water, where to find it and how to ensure its safety.

The need for water alone is a compelling reason for preparation. Anyone can think of numerous scenarios that could disrupt water and food supplies in the U.S. Therefore, if the possibility exists that the water supply to our homes could be disrupted, even if for a short period of time, then there is reason to maintain an emergency water supply and to learn how to obtain water from alternate sources if local services continue to be down.

SAFE WATER AND ITS SIGNIFICANCE

THE IMPORTANCE OF WATER

Water comprises about 70 percent of the human body (60 percent of our red blood cells and 80 percent of our muscle mass). Other than the air we breathe, water is the most common substance on the earth, but also the most vital.

Fresh water that we can use makes up less than 3 percent of the earth's total water volume. Most of the fresh water supply on the earth (80 percent) is in glacial ice and is therefore unavailable for our use. Approximately 15 percent of the fresh water supply is underground, with only 5 percent present as surface water such as lakes, rivers and streams.

THE IMPORTANCE OF STORING WATER

We need to know how to procure and store safe water. This was graphically illustrated only last year when the droughts occurring in Texas and Florida achieved prime-time news coverage. Also, there is an increasing outcry from people in cities such as Atlanta who have engaged in court battles about state water rights and the use of water.

Many people still recall the 1930s, when the farmlands of the Dakotas, eastern Colorado, parts of Kansas and Oklahoma were reduced to a dust bowl by drought and over farming. More recently, many countries, including the U.S., have had increasing problems with pollution of their water supplies, from flooding, silt, fertilizers and/or industrial waste. We should not wait for such widespread disasters to learn how to procure and store water for our loved ones and communities.

Your first priority in preparing for an emergency situation or for a long-term storage program is to learn about safe water storage and to implement a plan that ensures adequate amounts of safe water. Most diseases in developing nations today are infectious diseases caused by bacteria, viruses and other microbes from human feces polluting water used for drinking or washing. When people drink the water, the live microbes multiply, cause disease and set up a cycle of disease transmission.

In fact, unsafe water is a major problem worldwide. An estimated 1 billion people do not have access to safe water. It is estimated that diarrheal diseases kill about 2 million children and cause about 900 million episodes of illness each year.

SEVEN BASIC RECOMMENDATIONS

1. Store water from the source that you are currently using.
2. Store in clean, new, heavy-duty plastic containers with tight lids. A good container is available from the Department of Transportation (DOT No. 34).
3. Remember that water is heavy, weighing eight pounds per gallon. Therefore a five-gallon container weighs 40 pounds, and is the maximum weight most people can carry. This is the right size for water storage and stacking to conserve space. If you don't have a storage space problem, 55-gallon containers are available. However, once these plastic containers are filled they are difficult to move without being drained. The military uses inflatable rubber "water buffaloes" for troops on maneuvers that hold 5,000 to 10,000 gallons.
4. Don't use bottles to store water from foodstuffs that are alkaline or acidic, such as pickles or vinegar, because of the residual odor and taste.
5. Plastic is a permeable membrane that breathes, allowing contamination from strong odors and petroleum products. Therefore store your water away from all petroleum products, objectionable odors, animal waste and fertilizers.
6. Because water makes metal rust, don't store it in metal

containers unless there is a special coating of plastic or enamel on the inside.

7. Rotate your water supply. Water that has been stored properly in clean containers for several years cannot be distinguished in appearance, taste or odor from water recently drawn from the same source. However, the principle of rotation is the best guarantee for monitoring purity and taste.

TERMS YOU SHOULD KNOW

If you become serious about preparing to minister during a crisis, you will be reading material with terms that may be unfamiliar. Here is a mini-glossary of terms relating to water.

Potable water—Water that is safe for human consumption. It is free from disease-causing organisms and excessive amounts of mineral and organic matter, toxic chemicals and radioactivity.

Contaminated water—Water that is unfit for human consumption even though it may be pleasing to the taste (palatable). It may contain disease-causing organisms or excessive amounts of mineral and organic matter, toxic chemicals or radioactivity.

Palatable water—Water that is pleasing to the taste. As indicated above, however, not all palatable water is safe for human consumption.

Brackish water—Highly mineralized water that contains dissolved solids in excess of 500 ppm (parts per million; see below). It can be very alkaline or acidic. Brackish water is found in arid or semi-arid climates as groundwater, and along sea coasts.

Water treatment—The removal of undesirable constituents in water, normally through the processes of coagulation, sedimentation, filtration and/or disinfection.

Disinfection—Treatment with a chemical or by boiling to destroy disease-producing organisms.

Chlorination—Disinfection of water by the addition of a chlorine compound such as calcium hypochlorite.

Chlorine dosage—The amount of chlorine added to a given amount of water.

Chlorine residual—A tightly controlled measurement in water treatment plants to determine the level of chlorine compounds that kill bacteria without undue side effects.

Parts per million (ppm)—A unit of measurement for expressing the number of units of a substance in 1 million units of water, by weight.

Black water—Sewage water from human waste such as urine or feces.

Gray water—Water utilized for personal hygiene such as laundry, dish-washing and showers.

Surface water—Water available from lakes, streams, rivers and the oceans.

Groundwater—Water from wells and springs.

HOW MUCH FOR HOW LONG?

Subsistence level. This is the minimal daily amount of drinking water necessary to sustain normal body functions such as blood pressure, pulse and flushing out our kidneys. A minimum of two quarts of water are required daily. This does not allow for washing dishes or cleaning your body. High temperatures require greater amounts of water. Also, more water is usually needed for active children, nursing mothers and sick people.

Subsistence level in a hot, nonair-conditioned environment: one gallon per person per day.

Basic maintenance. This consists of the subsistence level (two quarts) plus basic personal needs such as cooking some food, brushing your teeth, and washing your face and hands—but no water for a bath or shower. Store at least two gallons of water for each member of your family for a minimum of two weeks. Thus, two gallons per day times four people times two weeks would equal 112 gallons.

For a family of four adults who have their food available in a dry form only, such as beans and rice, you would need at least one quart of water per meal for washing, soaking and cooking, thereby necessitating an additional three-fourths of a gallon per day for cooking. If you are expecting four people to be living in your home and relying on dry foods, the storage formula would be 8 gal./day x 14 days = 112 gal., x 2 weeks, + 10 gal. for dry food = 122 gal.

If you had no available water in your home, this would require at least 22 five-gallon containers or at least two 55-gallon plastic containers. Using these large containers would also require a siphon pump and a barrel cap wrench to remove water.

When dealing with larger numbers of people we can learn much from military standards for young recruits. Normal army provision in a work environment includes four gallons of water/person/day. A military "shower" is only 1.3 gallons/day, and is enough to wash your face and hands, brush your teeth and clean body areas that are prone to sweating: arm pits, groin and feet. (Proper allowances must be made for babies, small children, the elderly, the disabled or those requiring hospitalization with increased demands secondary to such things as diarrhea, dehydration or burn injuries.)

Field water supply for the military as seen in setting up a base camp for military personnel is dependent upon the season of the year, the geographical situation and the activities that are required. Dehydration can be a problem in both extremely hot and cold climates. More water is required for maintenance of personal hygiene and for reconstituting dehydrated foods.

In a warm, temperate climate the military allows for five gallons/man/day for drinking and cooking. When showering facilities are made available at a base camp, the amount required is 15 gallons/man/day. Therefore a soldier working in a warm climate who has a shower available learns to use no more than 20 gallons/day.

In contrast, the average American who has a washer, refrigerator, shower and/or bath tub, a four- to five-gallon flush toilet and a lawn irrigation system uses 50 gallons/water/day. An emergency that results in restricted water supplies would obviously require major changes in lifestyle!

TREATING CONTAMINATED WATER

BOILING WATER

The "gold standard" way to kill bacteria and other harmful organisms in water has been to boil the water at 100 degrees celsius or 212 degrees fahrenheit for 10 minutes at a rolling boil. Yet this is not uniformly practiced, for five main reasons:

1. People are ignorant of or do not believe in the germ theory of disease.
2. It takes too long.
3. Boiled water tastes bad.
4. Fuel is often limited or costly.
5. The heat and smoke are unpleasant.

To illustrate the impact of reason No. 4, during a cholera epidemic in Peru the Ministry of Health recommended that all residents boil water for 10 minutes. If everyone had instituted this program, the cost would have amounted to 29 percent of the average poor family's household income. In Bangladesh this would amount to 11 percent of the family income of people in the lower 25 percent income bracket. The city of Cebu, in the Philippines, has a population of 900,000, and about 50 percent of the population boil their drinking water. It takes about one kilogram of wood to boil one liter of water. Coal and coke are also used. This has led to deforestation and urban air pollution.

A SIMPLE WAY TO PASTEURIZE WATER

The pasteurization of water by solar cookers has been another way to kill germs. This is done by heating water to 65 degrees celsius for 30 minutes, or to 82 degrees celsius for a few seconds (or an intermediate temperature for an intermediate time). The most common causes of acute diarrhea in children in developing nations are the bacteria caused by Escheirichia coli and Shigella SD and the Rotavirus group of viruses. These are rapidly killed at temperatures of 60 degrees celsius or greater. Robert Metcalf, a Ph.D. microbiologist from Sacramento, California, has proved that water can be made safe to drink at a lower temperature—only 66 degrees celsius—instead of 100 degrees celsius.

A solar box cooker for pasteurizing water can be made by enclosing a dark water container in polyester (plastic) to create an insulating air space, and by using lots of reflectors to bounce light onto the jar. Dr. Metcalf can pasteurize one gallon of water in the summer in four hours with this simple system. The heated water can also be kept hot for a long time by placing it in its bag inside an insulated box. (See Solar Water Heating in chapter 12.)

DISINFECTING METHODS: ADVANTAGES
AND DISADVANTAGES

Chlorine. Throughout the world, and particularly in many developed nations, a variety of chlorine compounds are used to kill bacteria. In the U.S., approximately 80 to 85 percent of water treatment plants use chlorine derivatives after the water has been filtered. Chlorine is used in cities because of its availability and ease of use, and the advantage of sharing the cost. Most communities of 2,000 families and below cannot afford a $15 million water treatment plant.

Chemicals do not purify water; they render it drinkable by neutralizing some of the toxic animal and plant life in the water. The effectiveness of chlorine and iodine depends on the chemical concentration present, the length of time the chemical is in the water, the temperature of the water, the level of alkalinity and acidity present, and how clear or turbid the water is (the ratio of suspended particles in water). Colder water and water that is cloudy and turbid (with many dissolved particles present) require longer for the chlorine to kill the contaminants.

Water *treatment* is not the same as water *purification.* Water purification requires extensive treatment and processing, whereas water treatment chemicals are relatively inexpensive. In tablet, powder and concentrated liquid form, they are more portable than a bottle of bleach.

Sodium hypochlorite (5.25 percent solution) or household bleach without any soap or additives can be used to treat large amounts of water inexpensively. Household bleach normally is good for six months. Chlorine kills bacteria and most viruses. The concentration is as follows:

1 gallon—Add 8 drops for clear water, 16 if cloudy.
5 gallons—Add 1/2 tsp. for clear water, 1 tsp. if cloudy.

The disadvantage of chlorine is that it can combine with certain types of plastics used for containers, and has been determined to be a carcinogen when present in high levels. It is normal for someone to experience a chlorine taste to the water after it has been treated. One way to eliminate this taste is to mask it with something like Kool-Aid.

Iodine. In addition to chlorine, iodine is another chemical used to kill harmful organisms in water. Tincture of iodine is good for small quantities of water. The problem is that it has a peculiar taste and odor that some cannot tolerate. In fact, if you cannot taste the iodine or smell it after the water is treated, do not drink it because the iodine may have become weakened by time, heat or contamination. People who should not use iodine are pregnant or nursing mothers, and those with thyroid problems. The normal iodine treatment formula is:

1 gallon—Add 12 drops of 2 percent iodine if water is clear; double if water condition is cloudy.

Other Methods. Aerobic 07 is a chlorine-free electrolyte solution that releases extra single atoms of oxygen to water. Peroxide (H_2O_2) can kill certain bacteria, and has been used to clean out wounds that are infected. The method involves adding six drops to a gallon of water, and allowing the solution to stand for one hour (longer if water is cold, less time for warm or tepid water).

It should be noted, however, that on the flyer that accompanies Aerobic 07, the Aerobic Life Industries Company states that "We have not sponsored nor conducted sufficient scientific experiments to satisfy the guidelines of the FDA in order to be able to state any claims of this nature in our labeling, advertising literature or instructions." Until this occurs I cannot recommend this method.

FINDING ALTERNATIVE WATER SUPPLIES AROUND THE HOME

Could you find water in or around your home if the normal supply were cut off during a crisis? Here are some possibilities, some of which may surprise you.

PLUMBING

Hot water heaters normally contain 15 to 40 gallons of potable water, which is available simply by opening the drain faucet at the bottom the heater. You may need to screen or filter out sediment before drinking.

Tubs and sinks can be filled ahead of time when warnings make it possible to have additional water on hand. Toilet tanks (not toilet bowls) contain five to seven gallons. Always boil before using. If a disinfectant or cleaner is in the tank, the water will not be drinkable.

APPLIANCES

When possible, fill water coolers, clothes washer, tubs and buckets to capacity.

Water beds are controversial water sources. James Talmage Stevens (see resource list at the end of this chapter) recommends this source if the following precautions are followed. Using only a new mattress, fill with fresh tap water; add two ounces of bleach for 120 gallons of water; rotate water yearly. Boil water before using, and do not use toxic algae inhibitor solutions.

YARD AND GARDEN

Water hoses may contain good water, provided the end has not been in a bucket, barrel, ditch or puddle, and if the hose has not been used to siphon contaminated water.

Swimming pool and hot-water spas or hot tubs are another controversial source. They are preferable for storing water for nondrinking uses. If used for cooking and drinking, boil the water first.

SURFACE WATER

Water from lakes, streams, ponds and rivers should always be treated as contaminated water. Water may be filtered via sand, grass, charcoal, several layers of cloth or a field filtration unit like the military uses.

If you, your family or neighbors have to use surface water from a lake, find the cleanest source available. Make a sandy location one to six inches from the water's edge and dig a hole 12 inches below the water level. Wait for water to seep into the hole, allowing suspended particles to settle. Dip out clear water carefully to avoid transferring the mud. Then the water must be filtered to remove debris, and treated as contaminated.

CONSIDERATIONS FOR SELECTING A WATER SUPPLY FOR LARGER NUMBERS OF PEOPLE

In this section we will consider some of the same issues touched on above, but apply them to situations involving larger numbers of people. These suggestions would be useful in setting up a base camp, warehouse or other facility for your community.

Three general considerations in such situations are:

1. The water supply must be large enough for the quantity of people that are coming or expected taking into account the special needs required.

2. To minimize the amount of water treated, the water should be relatively unpolluted.
3. The water should be as easy as possible to obtain.

Think through a plan for utilizing the best sources of water in your community. Be aware of all possible contaminants in your area or region.

The Sept. 28, 1998, issue of *U.S. News and World Report* had an article entitled "Very Troubled Waters" that reported the results from the Clean Water Act in 1972, and where we are today in the U.S. The Clean Water Act made monumental progress in cleaning up American rivers. In 1972, only 30 to 40 percent of the rivers were suitable for fishing and swimming, compared to about 60 percent now.

However, progress has stagnated or possibly even backslid in the past decade. An analysis of Environmental Protection Agency (EPA) records from 1984 to 1998 reveals that the number of "impaired" rivers grew from 26 percent to 36 percent during that period. (A river is classified as impaired when it cannot support aquatic life or is unsafe for fishing or swimming.)

When the bill was passed in 1972 it was primarily for industrial plants and city sewers. It was not envisioned to handle today's pollutants: silt, bacteria, oxygen-depleting substances and pesticides. An area's location indicates the most common pollutants. In Mississippi, pesticides and bacteria are a serious problem; in Arizona, metal and salt; in Georgia, trash and fertilizers; in California, nutrients and silt from all the bridges and construction. In general, 70 percent of impaired rivers come from hog, poultry and cattle farm runoff containing manure, dirt and chemical fertilizers.

The article refers to a $2.3 billion Clean Water Action Plan released from the EPA and the Department of Agriculture, but pressure to weaken the regulations is coming from the agriculture industry. When there is an oversupply of nitrogen and phosphorous from fertilizer runoff, algae grows and dissolves oxygen in the water. The other major problem is construction. When a bridge is built over a river, displaced sediment can build up in the water.

THE THREE-STEP WATER TREATMENT METHOD
Providing large amounts of water requires:

1. *Clarification*—Filling large containers and leaving the water there until the undissolved solids settle to the bottom.
2. *Filtration*—Running the clarified water through a fine filter of sand or carbon material to remove undissolved solids.
3. *Disinfection*—Adding a chemical such as chlorine to the filtered water to kill harmful bacteria and organisms.

WATER PURIFIERS AND OTHER OPTIONS
Approximately 80 to 85 percent of water treatment plants use chlorine to kill bacteria after the water has been filtered. Because of the immense weight and bulk of large amounts of water that is stored for long intervals, even enough for a family of four, you will need to look into purifying your water by one or more alternative methods.

Almost all excellent water purifiers work on the principle of *reverse osmosis* or a *carbon filter*. These treatment methods help control lead poisoning from corroded pipes, which can cause brain damage, retarded development and permanent learning disabilities in children. The EPA estimates that 40 million people in the U.S. regularly drink water containing hazardous levels of lead.

Reverse osmosis also controls pollution from nitrates in fertilizer runoff, a condition occurring in 3 percent of households in the U.S. Many county health departments offer free, simple tests for three to five such impurities. (If you want to check for other ingredients in your water, *Lehman's Non-Electric Catalog* lists two companies that will test your water for a cost of $130 to $170. See the resource list at the end of this chapter.)

"Crypto," or cryptosporidiosis, is a diarrheal disease caused by a protozoa in some water. It is seen in people who are weak, debilitated and have a compromised immune system. This disease can occur all over the world in children, travelers to developing nations, and medical personnel caring for these patients. It can be transmitted by drinking contaminated water.

All bacterial contamination in water can be controlled by a Katadyn filter. It is reported by *Lehman's* to be the only filter that always stops germs, parasites, cysts and bacteria. It protects against typhoid, dysentery, cholera and "traveler's diarrhea" or giardiasis.

Untreated water does not get past this type of filter. The water flow decreases when it is time to clean the element. The filter pores are extremely small, actually microscopic (0.2 microns). Silver granules sealed in the filter prevent bacterial growth and mold. The filter contains no chemicals such as chlorine or iodine. EPA approved, it removes 100 percent of algae, suspended contaminants and bacteria. These Swiss-made filters are used by NATO, the Red Cross and Wycliffe Bible Translators. The filters can treat up to 13,000 gallons before the element must be replaced.

For individual and particularly travel use, you can purchase a portable Katadyn that is smaller than a large flashlight, through *Lehman's Catalog.* This pocket-size model is fast and long-lasting, and is ideal for serious expeditions. It has a tough plastic cylinder encased in indestructible cast aluminum, and comes with a lifetime warranty.

The Katadyn Drip Filter is the easiest to use to produce safe drinking water and cooking water indoors or outside. It uses gravity pressure to produce up to 12 gallons of clear water per day. Untreated water drips from the top container into the bottom at a rate of one-half gallon per hour. This model removes all harmful bacteria and micro-organisms down to 0.2 microns. It comes with 21 low-pressure ceramic filtering elements, which will filter up to 26,000 gallons.

The Katadyn Combi Filter uses a dual filtration system consisting of a ceramic filter plus an activated charcoal filter which not only eliminates bacteria and micro-organisms but also chlorine, iodine, odors and bad tastes. The ceramic element will filter up to 14,000 gallons of water. The activated carbons will filter up to 60 gallons before needing to be replaced. This type of filter can be used without carbon granulate if desired.

SURFACE AND GROUNDWATER

When a disaster destroys the usual public water supply system it is important to search for large amounts of water supplies that are independent of the usual public water supply system.

SURFACE WATER
Water from nearby lakes or streams can be obtained for large

groups of people by various means. Here are three ways to obtain water from such sources:

1. Float or stake an inlet hose to the water. A hose with a strain filter on the end is tied to the middle of a post or pile, which is pushed into the bottom of the lake bed. The filter will mean that less mud and sedimentation will have to be removed.

2. Another option is to bury a hose in the bottom of a gravel-filled pit in the bottom of a stream or lake. The coarse gravel surrounding the filter on the end of the hose will also help to eliminate the sediment from the water.

3. The third option is to float a 55-gallon metal drum that is anchored to the bottom of a lake bed or a fast-moving stream. A hose with an intake screen is fastened to lines beneath the floating metal drum. The hose in turn is connected to a pump for water removal.

COLLECTING RAIN WATER OR SNOW

Precipitation from rain or snow can provide water if caught in clean containers, and may be used without treatment. All water caught in bowls, pans, buckets, barrels and storage cisterns should be treated. During a heavy rainstorm, 40 to 50 gallons of water can be collected quickly if your drainage gutters are clean and able to drain into a container such as a 55-gallon drum or a plastic cistern. Shake-shingle and other wooden roofs are not good for this. If you are unsure of the composition of your roof and need to collect rain water, cover the side of the roof that you want to collect it from with a clean plastic tarp that will drain into your gutter and collection device.

The first snow to fall contains environmental contaminants. Collect later, clean-fallen snow as a clean water source. For old snow, remove the crust, and use the protected snow underneath for clean water use. If unsure of quality, treat as contaminated.

GROUNDWATER

If you are unable to obtain surface water that is suitable for your needs, then you may need to consider drilling a well. However, when you do this you must be aware of who owns the water rights where you live. In the U.S., this varies from state to state and even within the states.

If you can drill, you should find out the depth of the water table before you start. The well needs to be deep enough to allow for a "drawdown" of the well water with repeated use.

A well must be large enough to provide everyone with more water than they will need. In the event of a power shortage, you will need to have a hand pump, a generator, a solar pump or a windmill to make the well work effectively without electricity. If water is more than 175 feet down, the water soon becomes too heavy to pump by hand for any length of time.

Water from a well should not be considered safe until it is tested by a county health or sanitation department, which takes a water sample and sends you a report based on its purity. For more information on this I recommend that you obtain *Lehman's Catalog* and/or the *Jade Mountain Appropriate Technology for Sustainable Living*, 1998 catalog (see the resource list at the end of the chapter).

WASTE AND OTHER SANITATION CONCERNS

HANDLING GARBAGE AND SEWAGE

During emergencies, expect delays in garbage collection. Rodents can be a major health threat where garbage accumulates. Waste water and sewage treatment plants are highly automated, and environmental monitoring and control systems depend on computers with embedded controls that are vulnerable to "hackers." Pump station networks that monitor sewage and waste-water flows may be affected by emergencies as well as by flooding.

To prepare for such contingencies, be sure that you have sturdy, lidded containers to hold refuse over a two-week period. Don't allow garbage to accumulate outside your home. In rural areas, trash can be attractive to some dangerous wildlife.

Most toilets that are used in homes have a three- to five-gallon capacity. When a water shortage is expected or present, fill up the bath tub ahead of time. This should provide enough water to clean out the toilet bowl after use for a week or more. Bleach can be used to deodorize and disinfect the toilet.

Because water and sewage are affected by gravity, people living in low-lying or flood-prone areas may have their sewage system backed up into their sinks and water pipes. If you hear an unusual gurgling sound in your pipes, you may be in for an unpleasant backup of water and ultimately sewage on your carpet and floors. This happened to a good friend of ours who is a civil engineer, and who owned some rental property. In these low-lying areas this civil engineer recommends that you close your bathroom sinks and try to close up all the holes with rubber, plastic or cork plugs.

To understand waste disposal, it is helpful to learn some military terms and observe how the army handles waste. The military is trained for mobility, handling large numbers in a relatively short period of time, camp cleanliness and personal hygiene for the good of the whole. The methods the military use depend on the duties required of the unit and their location. They have learned that when wastes are not quickly disposed of the area quickly becomes a breeding ground for flies, rats and other vermin. Filth-borne diseases such as dysentery, typhoid, cholera and plague can become prevalent. The military describes four types of waste.

HUMAN WASTE

Long ago, the Bible indicated an awareness of the capacity of human feces and urine to contaminate. During their wandering in the wilderness, the children of Israel were commanded: "You shall also have a place outside the camp and go out there, and you shall have a spade among your tools, and it shall be when you sit down outside, you shall dig with it and shall turn to cover up your excrement" (Deut. 23:12,13, *NASB*).

In a normal situation a person releases approximately one gallon of waste products daily. When people are on the move, they should have a shovel or similar device for each person to use a "cat hole" latrine. This is simply a hole one foot deep, which is completely covered and packed down after use.

For temporary camps, a *straddle trench* can be used until a more permanent facility is made (see diagram below).

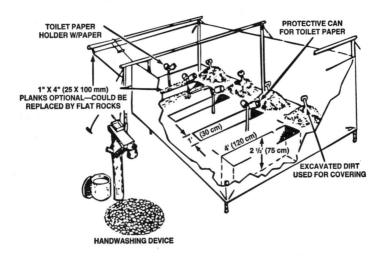

A straddle trench dug one foot wide, two feet deep and four feet long will accommodate two men at the same time. There should be enough to accommodate 8 percent of the people at one time. For example, there should be eight saddle trenches for 100 people. The earth is removed and replaced at one end. A shovel is placed there so that the excreta and toilet paper can be covered after each use.

A *deep-pit latrine* with a urine soakage pit is constructed for longer periods of time. It is usually less than six feet deep, and about two feet wide and seven feet long. It has four seats that are closed with fly-proof, self-closing lids. All cracks are closed by pieces of wood or metal to prevent flies.

A *burn-out latrine* may be used when the soil conditions are hard, frozen, or rocky, or where there are high water tables. It cannot be used where air pollution regulations prohibit open fires. A 55-gallon metal drum is placed in the ground, leaving enough of the drum above the ground for a comfortable sitting height. The drum may be cut in half to provide two such seats.

A wooden seat with a fly-proof, self-closing lid is placed on the top of the drum. Urine from the men is hopefully placed in a separate facility because more fuel is required to burn the liquid urine. This type of latrine is burned out daily with a mixture of one quart of gasoline to five quarts of diesel oil. This needs to be done carefully. Gasoline is too explosive in nature to be used alone. If the contents are not rendered dry and odorless with one burning, they should be burned again. The remaining dry ash should be buried.

Considering that a normal healthy adult releases about a gallon of waste per day, a family of four people, over a two-week period, would need to be able to eliminate 56 gallons of urine or feces in a safe manner away from your water supply.

When handling large numbers of displaced people, such as refugees, the following safety rules for construction, maintenance and closing of latrines are essential for life and health:

1. To protect the groundwater from contamination, be sure that the depth of the urine pit is well above the underground water level.
2. The latrine should be at least 100 yards away from the kitchen and from the nearest water source.
3. Choose a locale that is accessible to users but near the perimeter of the base camp site.
4. Place something like canvas or brush around the latrine sites.
5. To prevent surface water from flowing into the latrine areas, dig drainage ditches around them.
6. Provide toilet paper on suitable holders with tin cans for covering them to keep the paper from getting wet during bad weather.
7. Install a simple hand-washing device outside the latrine shelter, with enough water for each person to wash his hands after using the latrine.
8. Keep the lids to the latrine seats closed at all times, and maintain a good fly-control program to prevent breeding and reduce odors.
9. Scrub the latrine seats and boxes daily with soap and water.
10. Spray the inside of the shelters with insecticide twice weekly.

When the latrine contents are up to a foot from the surface, or the latrine is to be abandoned, remove the barrel or box and apply insecticide to the contents, side walls and the ground surface two feet from the side walls. Fill the pit to ground level with successive three-inch layers of earth, packing down each layer before applying the next. Then mound the pit over with one foot of dirt, and spray again with insecticide. This will prevent fly larvae from hatching and causing contamination.

LIQUID WASTES FROM BATH AND KITCHEN

The handling of liquid waste for larger numbers is also important to know in the event of emergencies. Waste water from kitchens, showers and laundries must be routed through a grease pit, which removes the soap and grease and allows the water to evaporate in a soakage pit or a lagoon. If the soil where you live is relatively porous (like sand), waste water can be disposed of in a soakage pit. Otherwise, a large area downwind from the camp is required for an open-air lagoon.

In a temporary situation, a soakage pit four feet square and four feet deep will normally dispose of wash and kitchen wastes. Otherwise, an evaporation bed may be used if the climate is hot and dry. Every place where there is washing and bathing must have a soakage pit beneath it.

The area under field showers should be excavated a few inches, then filled with small, smooth stones to keep the water from standing. To understand more about soakage pits and grease traps, I refer you to military manuals which go into this in greater detail.

GARBAGE DISPOSAL

On maneuvers, the military usually disposes of garbage—the solid or semi-solid waste resulting from the preparation, cooking and serving of food—by burying it in pits or trenches. Here are some methods and safety guidelines:

1. Pits should not be more than 30 yards from the food preparation site, but must not be buried closer than 100 feet to any source of water used for cooking or drinking.
2. A useful pit size is four feet square and four feet deep.
3. For longer periods of time, a longer trench is dug. When additional trenches are required, the excavated dirt from previous pits is used to cover and mound the garbage already deposited.
4. Pits should be sprayed with insecticide at the end of each day.
5. When almost filled, they should be closed with impacted earth.
6. Garbage can also be handled by incineration where allowed.

SOLID WASTE RUBBISH DISPOSAL

Solids will also have to be disposed of in a sanitary manner. These wastes include rubbish such as cans and boxes, ashes and, at times, industrial waste. Care is taken to flatten tin cans and break down boxes before they are added to the rubbish. Combustible rubbish is usually burned in a barrel incinerator. Non-combustible rubbish is either buried or hauled to a suitable site where hopefully it can be covered by a landfill.

Plan for the disposal of four pounds of rubbish per person per day, either by burning or burial. Burning as much as possible will greatly reduce the volume to be buried.

A barrel incinerator can be made from a 55-gallon drum with the top and bottom removed.

Perforations or holes are placed in numerous locations near the bottom of the barrel. Metal grates are inserted inside the barrel several inches above the holes. The metal drum is lifted up and placed several inches above the ground on bricks or stones or metal cans filled with soil, and a fire is lit underneath. The rubbish is put into the barrel on the top grate.

SUMMARY CHECKLIST: WHERE DO WE GO FROM HERE?

1. In an attitude of prayer, not fear, assess the current spiritual climate of your region and observe the number of crises that have been occurring with floods, hurricanes, tsunamis or tidal waves, droughts, economic downturns with loss of jobs and deflation, computer problems secondary to the computer millennium bug, and the potential of man-made disasters from chemical and biological warfare.

2. Ask the Lord for guidance in determining the potential for such calamities that could occur in your region, and their effects on your loved ones, your church and your community.

3. Determine how your loved ones, church and community are preparing for these events.

4. Ask the Lord how long you and your area could be without adequate water availability, sewer capability, or garbage pickup and disposal. Select one of the following: 2 weeks___ 2 months___ 6 months___ 12 months___.

5. Other than yourself, in the event of a crisis, how many people would be looking to you for help and advice? 1 person___ 2 people___ 4___ 8___ more___.

6. What would be the duration of these events? Make the following calculations: For a typical family of four or a church of 100 members for two months. For a family

of four at only basic maintenance (two gallons/person/day), you must store 240 gallons of water or have additional methods of water collection and purification. For a church, store 6,000 gallons or have additional methods of collection such as a well on site.

7. In the event that additional types of water containers and/or water purifiers and/or wells are needed for the timeline you have selected, what contingency plans have you, your family and your group made to be prepared to share with others?

May God guide you in making reasonable assessments and making wise plans in your own situation. In the well-known proverb, even the lowly ant is praised for storing up provisions and making adequate preparation (Prov. 6:6-8). In view of the increasing number of crises all about us, can Christians do less?

RESOURCES

Back to Basics. Pleasantville, NY: Reader's Digest, 1992.

Dale, Andreatta, Ph.D. "A Summary of Water Pasteurization Techniques." Available from www.accessone.com/sbcn/solarwat.html; INTERNET.

Gill, Capt. Heidi Falk, civil/structural engineer, U.S. Air Force Engineering Corp. "Field Water Supply." Tulsa, OK: International Health Services Foundation Lecture Series, January 1995.

High, David. *Y2K Preparedness Booklet.* Oklahoma City: Millennial Technologies, 1998. Tel. 405-478-4351.

Hovel, Happy. "The Keeping of Water." Available from http//:www.happyhovel.com; INTERNET; or tel. 1-800-637-7772.

Jade Mountain Appropriate Technology for Sustainable Living, 1998 Catalog. P.O. Box 4616, Boulder, CO 80306-4616; e-mail: info@jademountain.com. *Lehman's Non-Electric Catalog.* Tel. 330-857-5757; fax: 330-857-5785; e-mail: GetLehmans@aol.com.

O'Riley, Paloma. *Individual and Community Preparation for Y2K.* Louisville, CO: The Cassandra Project, 1998. Available from http://millennia-bcs.com/casframe.htm; INTERNET.

Settle, Joe. Professional civil engineer and lecturer for the International Health Services Foundation Lecture Series, Tulsa, OK.

Stevens, James Talmage. *Making the Best of the Basics,* 10th ed. Salt Lake City: Gold Leaf Press, 1997.

Winn, Richard. "Water Problems?" Available from http://www.homestead.org; INTERNET.

MEDICAL CONCERNS IN TIMES OF CRISIS

MARK NEUENSCHWANDER, M.D.

In this chapter we will look first at plans you need to make to treat your family for minor medical problems in an emergency, whether they are the peculiar health challenges that Y2K may present or the normal things that one should at least think through in the case of natural disasters. We will also refer you to good sources that you might consider for health management of larger-scale problems involving more people, and describe some pitfalls and suggestions related to stockpiling pharmaceuticals for local or international use. Finally you will be given an overview of chemical and biological warfare, the agents that have been used in the past, and issues we need to prayerfully consider in the future.

PERSONAL AND FAMILY HEALTH CONCERNS

MEDICAL KITS

Every person living alone and every family should have a good medicine kit. If cost is a crucial consideration, I recommend the list compiled by The Cassandra Project with Paloma O'Riley, and the list thoughtfully compiled by James Talmage Stevens in his previously mentioned book, *Making the Best of Basics,* as good examples.

The problem that most of us have is that we normally do not have or take the time to methodically go through and buy all the items that should be in a well-stocked medicine kit. Although I am board certified and residency trained in two medical specialties, I did not begin this journey with a complete kit. Instead, I have taken the advice of others and purchased different types of first-aid kits that are readily available.

The first is a Comprehensive Plus Kit, which contains over 180 items and is useful for both novices and seasoned Emergency Medical Technicians. It comes in a convenient water-resistant, nylon zipped pouch with the contents in plastic bags for protection.

Another recommended kit is the Knuckle Mender II First Aid Kit, which has 60 items that fit easily into a 72-hour travel bag. This kit has items for treating a variety of ailments, including minor cuts and scrapes, splinters, burns, insect stings, blisters, sunburn, headaches, upset stomach and much more. We also purchased the Dental First-Aid Kit, which helps handle dental emergencies including lost fillings.

If you were to foresee being in a major crisis where medical facilities are not immediately available or where they will be dealing with major trauma themselves, you might want to consider an Advanced Suture and Syringe Kit. This kit provides essentials needed to perform minor surgery or suturing with sterile supplies. We purchased these kits through Don McAlvany's International Collections Associate Center in Durango, Colorado.

An excellent book that we and our teams have used in India to teach rural health care to Bible school students is produced by the

Hesperian Foundation, P.O. Box 1692, Palo Alto, CA. It is called *Where There Is No Doctor*, and was written by David Werner. It is not written from a Christian perspective, but is available in many languages and is loaded with practical points. Topics include "How to Examine a Sick Person," "Right and Wrong Use of Medicines," "First Aid," "Nutrition: What to Eat to Be Healthy," "Common and Serious Sicknesses" and treatment of problems involving skin, eyes, teeth and gums, and the urinary system.

HEALTH CHALLENGES FROM Y2K

Special problems may occur in the health-care industry with the Y2K bug, or millennium computer problem. Like most businesses, your pharmacy maintains its records on computers, and they are subject to the same problems as other businesses. If you or members of your family take medication regularly, ask your doctor for an additional prescription ahead of time, to be used elsewhere if your regular pharmacy experiences any problems or delays. You may need to pay for this in cash, if Y2K results in other problems with credit cards or transfers of funds. After receiving your prescription, inspect carefully for any errors in your name, the drug name, dosage, quantity and expiration.

I would try to avoid all elective surgery in the early part of the year 2000. If elective surgery needs to be done, I recommend that you have it before the end of 1999. In the event of an emergency, it is possible that malfunctioning telephones could make it impossible for an ambulance to be dispatched to a person in need. You need to think through how to transport yourself or someone else to the nearest emergency facility.

If you or members of your family are dependent on medical devices, it is important to contact the manufacturer and obtain in writing their assurance that the device will function properly after the year 2000. Consult your physician about any alternatives that would be available in an emergency. Devices that may be affected by Y2K problems include intravenous drip pumps, heart defibrillators, pacemakers, ICU monitors, CT scans, dialysis machines, chemotherapy and radiation equipment, laboratory and other diagnostic systems, and some monitoring and control systems dealing with the environment and with equipment safety.

The frail, elderly people with particular medical problems need a caregiver to perform daily tasks, and people with handicaps must make special plans in the event of Y2K-related problems. For example, this could apply to acute or chronic breathing problems, heart ailments, unstable or juvenile diabetes, dependence on tube feeding, epilepsy, tracheostomies, urinary catheters, colostomies and dialysis.

HANDLING PHARMACEUTICALS BEFORE AND DURING DISASTERS

A basic knowledge of the material in this section will be helpful for anyone who desires to help others in times of disasters, whether it be flood victims from Hurricane Mitch in Central America or victims of a natural disaster in your own community whom you or your church leaders want to assist. The following suggestions have proved to be timely and cost-effective in avoiding contamination and waste.

Small packages of pharmaceuticals that have been presorted and properly labeled are of great benefit. Packages should be prelabeled with field conditions in mind. Weather-resistant labels in the local languages, generic names, quantities, expiration dates, and international coding (green for medical supplies and equipment, red for food, blue for clothing) should be used whenever possible. Be careful not to use expired pharmaceuticals. This problem can be serious in the case of some drugs; for example, the common antibiotic tetracycline. Using expired tetracycline can cause kidney damage.

Occasionally overpacking is a problem. If you are sending pharmaceuticals to a humid environment in a tropical country, pack with a desiccant (drying agent). Insulin and some vaccines do not tolerate temperature extremes.

Remember that the type and phase of a disaster dictate what medications are needed; and that the local or regional area that has suffered a severe disaster is the one that usually supplies pharmaceuticals. During the recovery phase of most disasters, victims may have difficulty accessing physicians and pharmaceutical services for ongoing medical care. Another problem can be the lack of access to patient records. Treatment of routine acute and chronic conditions is the mainstay of health-care relief efforts during the recovery phase of any type of disaster.

Following Hurricane Andrew, which was accompanied by 1,500 patient encounters, there was quick depletion of tetanus toxoid, antibiotics and insulin within 24 hours. Replacement of these supplies and medications to refill prescriptions were the most pressing needs.

When massive evacuations are required, some common problems encountered are sunburn, dehydration and motion sickness. This was particularly seen with the Mt. Pinatubo eruption in the Philippines, in close proximity to Clark Air Force Base. However, the vast majority of pharmaceuticals given at that time were for routine and chronic medical diagnoses.

Generally speaking, the most common drugs and items needed in the first phase of disaster recovery are antibiotics, tetanus toxoid, insulin, analgesics for pain relief, cardiac medications, anticonvulsants, rehydration fluids, cold preparations and contraceptives.

BIOLOGICAL AND CHEMICAL WARFARE

This last century has been marked by several episodes of the use of weapons of mass destruction—not just against soldiers but innocent civilians as well. Even before the planned use of biological weapons in this century, history records some startling realities.

In the area of biological disasters, the epidemic of the bubonic plague, carried by fleas on rats, killed an estimated 25 percent of the population in Europe (25 million) between 1347 and 1351. The introduction of smallpox into the New World by European explorers decimated the Native American population. Between the years of 1918 to 1919, 50 million people worldwide were killed by the Spanish flu. In World War I, German agents inoculated horses bound for France with bacteria that caused the disease known as glanders infection. And in 1940, Japanese planes dropped chemical agents on China that cause bubonic plague.

In an example of chemical warfare, Italy used mustard gas as a weapon of mass destruction against Ethiopia in 1935–36. Japan is known to have used mustard gas and chlorine gas in China during the period of 1930–44. Egypt is reported to have used mustard gas against Yemen in 1957–63. In Afghanistan the Soviets used lethal chemical agents from 1977–89. And in the Iran-Iraq war of 1978–89, both sides used nerve and mustard agents.

The chemical agents called G agents are primarily nerve gases that are "organophosphate" substances and function like a pesticide. The route of exposure is either through inhalation or through the skin (cutaneous exposure). The normal nerve-to-muscle function in our bodies occurs at a receptor by the release of a substance called acetylcholine. Too much of this substance, or the inability for it to be controlled or neutralized by acetylcholinesterase, prevents the muscle from relaxing, thus causing it to be continually stimulated.

Thus the G or chemical warfare agents in low doses produce increased salivation, runny nose, chest tightness, nausea and hallucinations. In moderate doses people begin to cough, have difficulty breathing, muscle tremors, weakness and convulsions. In higher doses people convulse, lose consciousness, have muscular paralysis and die by suffocation.

Impairment from most chemical agents such as Tabun, Sarin, GF and VX can be treated by one to two mgs. of atropine into the muscle with an autoinjector. This stops the stimulation of the receptors inhibiting the transmission of excess amounts of acetylacholine. This medication, however, cannot be repeatedly given. Another drug called Prelidoxime administered in 600-mg. intramuscular or intravenous doses may be repeatedly given. It works by a different mechanism but with the same result.

Mustard gas attacks the system either by inhalation or skin absorption. This chemical produces severe skin and respiratory burns, with eye damage as well. It is very debilitating and has been used basically to paralyze enemy troops.

Biological agents include bacteria, rickettsia, viruses and toxins that can induce illness or death. They can be produced easily and at relatively low cost. Biological agents are many times deadlier, pound for pound, than chemical agents. Ten grams of anthrax spores could kill as many people as a ton of the nerve agent Sarin. Normally the effects of chemical agents occur within seconds of exposure, as in the case of nerve and blood agents, or as long as several hours with mustard gas administered in low doses.

BIOLOGICAL AND CHEMICAL COMPARISONS

Except in cases of exposure to a toxin, biological agents may not result in symptoms or death for several days or even weeks. This biological incubation time is the period necessary for the biological agent to establish itself and multiply in the individual infected.

One biological agent does not require an incubation period. This is a substance called botulinus, which releases a toxin that is the most toxic substance known to man. Without supportive care, inhaling only a very small amount of nanograms of this substance will cause progressive paralysis leading to asphyxiation and death.

Chemical agents are released either in a vapor or a liquid method. Soldiers are protected from this by wearing a protective mask and the MOPP (mission-oriented protective posture) suit. In contrast, biological agents work through an inhalation route, and the most effective way to release it is through an aerosol in the 105-micron particle size. An invisible aerosol cloud may be efficiently created using an agricultural sprayer. The current U.S. military protective mask, when properly fitted, affords 100-percent protection.

Currently it is difficult to detect when biological agents are being used. Vaccines, immunoglobulins and antibiotics can decrease the effect of biological agents. All three types of products can provide protection before and after the agent is released. Several problems, however, are often encountered. Most vaccines are highly specific against particular agents, thus not affording protection against the variety that could be used by an enemy. Also, it may take 10 to 15 years to develop a safe vaccine suitable for human use. Several vaccines are effective against botulinum toxin and tularemia, but they have not been FDA approved and are still in investigational new drug status.

Furthermore, even after a vaccine is developed there is a lag time before adequate protective antibodies develop. In addition, a sufficiently high dose of a biological agent or infectious disease can overwhelm any vaccine. Immunoglobulins do not stimulate active production of antibodies, and provide only short-term protection—usually lasting weeks or months. Immunoglobulins also require rigorous FDA approval.

WEAPONIZING BIOLOGICAL WARFARE

Both chemical and biological agents can be weaponized into conventional munitions by artillery rounds, cluster bombs and missile warheads. In general, biological agents are sensitive to environmental stress. Excessive heat, ultraviolet light, humidity and oxidation decrease their potency. They can be commercially available in agricultural sprayers. Thus unmanned, remotely piloted vehicles with spray tanks could be used.

We can compare the lethality of a biological agent in contrast to a chemical agent by comparing Sarin (used in the Tokyo subway) with anthrax. Releasing 1,000 kilograms of the nerve agent Sarin under mild to moderate winds at night would affect 7.8 square miles. In Washington, D.C., this would kill 3,000 to 8,000 people. In contrast, only one-tenth as much anthrax, or 100 kilograms, would cover 300 square kilometers and result in 1 to 3 million deaths. Anthrax, under proper conditions, could kill as many people as a nuclear device.

Inhaled anthrax (also known as Woolsorters' disease) spores are difficult to kill. They can survive in the soil and on water surfaces for years. Anthrax victims initially come to the emergency rooms with flu-type symptoms: mild fever, fatigue, muscle aches, nonproductive coughing and chest pressure. This phase can last for several days. Then suddenly people have severe shortness of breath, hypotension, cyanosis (turning blue in color), and go into shock. This last phase usually lasts less than 24 hours and ends in death, despite therapy. The standard therapy has been to give penicillin intravenously, and if necessary, the expensive drug Vancomycin.

THE CURRENT THREAT

Such weapons of mass destruction are located in the most unstable parts of the world—the Middle East, South Asia and on the Korean Peninsula. Iraq has disclosed that between 1985 and 1991 it produced two germ-warfare agents, anthrax and botulinum toxin. To a third-world nation, germ warfare is considered a great equalizer in comparison to other nations. Biotechnology allows small facilities to produce large amounts of biological agents. Ten million dollars allows someone to produce a large arsenal of them.

Eight nations have been implicated in developing offensive biological warfare capabilities: Iran, Iraq, Israel, North Korea, China, Libya, Syria and Taiwan. Also, Russia has admitted to developing an offensive program in violation of the Biological Weapons Convention.

During Operation Desert Storm, Iraq capitalized on the allied bombing of a suspected weapons factory by calling it only a "baby milk facility" for propaganda purposes. CNN's Peter Arnett's visit to the site raised public doubts about whether this was a legitimate Allied target, when in fact, it was. The Iraqi experience proves that biological warfare programs can exist and be hidden within legitimate facilities. Even direct, on-site visits may not reveal the existence of a facility capable of producing chemical and biological agents for warfare unless the visitors know exactly where to go and are permitted entry.

Thus, current threats to use chemical and biological agents against the U.S. are very real. The former assistant chief paramedic for the Chicago Fire Department has written that many U.S. fire/police/paramedic chiefs are aware of the implications of a terrorist attack or a major accident involving chemical or biological weapons. However, most acknowledge that during current government downsizing, as of spring 1999, they don't have budgets for training personnel or buying equipment that would be necessary to effectively prepare for the threat.

Some administrators are doing nothing, believing that the federal government will step in with large supplies of antidotes. Emergency preparedness experts, however, say that the arrival of supplies and personnel from other agencies might be so delayed as to prove ineffectual to assist those who are poisoned. Some other administrators, without actually purchasing the potentially large quantities of antidotes and decontamination agents, have made prior arrangements to obtain bulk stores of specific antidotes from local distributors on a 24-hour-a-day basis. This scenario of "just in time" procurement of essential supplies could be a potential, horrific problem if compounded by computer millennium bug challenges.

INTERCESSION AS A DEFENSE

It is imperative that Christians pray to the Lord for the leaders of our countries, as the apostle Paul urged: "I urge, then, first of all, that requests, prayers, intercession and thanksgiving be made for everyone—for kings and all those in authority, that we may live peaceful and quiet lives in all godliness and holiness" (1 Tim. 2:1,2).

Mike and Cindy Jacobs are the founders of a group called Generals of Intercession and they coordinate the U.S. Spiritual

Warfare Network. Cindy stated in early 1999, in two conversations with me, that she believes that if it were not for such intercessors, America would have already been attacked with major releases of chemical and biological agents. It is imperative that we pray, building up ourselves and others in the most holy faith. We need to build up our spiritual storehouse of scriptures (see chapter 7 and appendix IV) for protection and for divine health.

RESOURCES

Boyls, Kathy, M.D., FAAP. "Emergency Pediatric Encachment for Large Groups of People." Paper presented to the IHSF Disaster Relief Graduates and Faculty, 1998.

Celentano, John, M.D., EMS. "Chemical and Biological Agent Overview" Lecture presented in a medical forum on "Life Saving Intervention," Denver, CO, 1998.

Clinical Treatment Protocols for Chemical/Biological Warfare. 1996 Olympic Guidelines.

Greiser, William, M.D., FACS, IHSF. "Emergency Medical Encachment for Larger Groups of People." Paper presented to the IHSF Disaster Relief Graduates and Faculty, 1998.

Kaklec, Lt. Col. Robert P., USAF. "Twenty-First Century Germ Warfare," chap. 9 in Battlefield of the Future. Available from http://www.emergency.com/chemattk.htn; INTERNET.

Lacy, Elizabeth, D.O., R.Ph. "Pharmaceutics in Disasters," Disaster Medicine. August 1998.

O'Riley, Paloma. Individual and Community Preparation for Y2K. Louisville, CO: The Cassandra Project, 1998. Available from http://millennia-bcs.com/casframe.htm; INTERNET.

Sidell, Frederick R., M.D. *Medical Management of Chemical Warfare Agent Causalities: A Handbook for Emergency Medical Services.* Bel Air, MD: HB Publishing, 1995. P. O. Box 902, Bel Air, MD 21014.

Staten, Clark. *Chemical Attack—Are We Prepared?* Available from http://www.emergency.com/chemattk.htn; INTERNET.

Stevens, James Talmage. *Making the Best of the Basics.* Salt Lake City: Gold Leaf Press, 10th ed., 1997.

ALTERNATE FUELS, ENERGY SOURCES AND COMMUNICATIONS

DON LARSON, ELECTRICAL ENGINEER

One winter in Colorado a blizzard kept us in our house for three days. What happened next I believe was God's way of showing me the necessity of preparation for Y2K and other disasters. The fan motor on our furnace happened to fail just as the blizzard began. Because of the snow, the repairman could not get to our house for three days to fix the motor. After sending two members of the family to a neighbor's house to stay warm, my two sons and I donned our heaviest coats and decided to tough it out. Although we had electricity, the furnace could not heat the house. So we turned on the oven, left the door open and at least kept the pipes in the house from freezing.

Had there been an electrical failure it would have been worse, because I would not have had the electric stove to keep the temperature above freezing. I would have had to drain the pipes in the whole house, as well as the water standing in the drain system (sink traps, toilet tank and bowl) to keep them from bursting.

We are so accustomed to flipping a light switch, and relying on the furnace with automatic thermostat that we seldom consider alternative energy sources. Yet all of us have experienced episodes of energy failures for short periods of time. The problem, of course, is what we would do if these outages were long-term and widespread.

This chapter on alternative fuel and energy sources will focus on preparing your home so you can help yourself and others whom you may need to accommodate in your home in case of an extended utility failure. The ideas here can be expanded and applied to shelters for large groups, such as churches, schools, civic centers, etc. They are intended to help us obey Paul's command in Galatians 6:10: "Therefore, as we have opportunity, let us do good to all people, especially to those who belong to the family of believers."

THE ENERGY WE NEED

Of course our most urgent need for energy during an emergency is met by the regenerating power of the Holy Spirit. It is reassuring to know that in every situation we have access to the universe's ultimate Source of energy. It is out of this power that we can do all things through Christ, who strengthens us (see Phil. 4:13).

Humanly speaking, we use energy in **four primary areas** of our lives: **heating, cooking, lighting,** and for **electrical appliances,** such as refrigerators, washers, hair dryers, TVs, etc.

HEATING

The first two types of heating listed in table I, gas and electric furnaces, would both be inoperative in a crisis that knocks out the electricity or gas supply to the home. As an alternative, in areas of the U.S. that have an abundant supply of wood or coal, a wood-burning or coal-burning stove makes the best investment. I have a neighbor who has heated his entire house with a wood-burning stove for 20 years, using three cords of wood each winter.

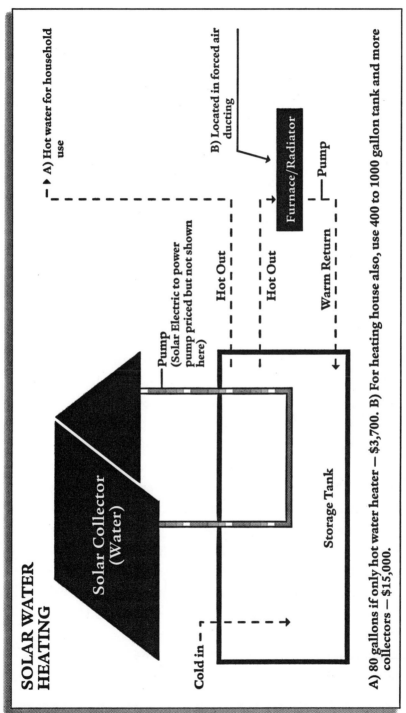

SOLAR WATER HEATING

Solar Collector (Water)

Pump (Solar Electric to power pump priced but not shown here)

Cold in ➔

Storage Tank

Hot Out

Hot Out

Warm Return

Pump

Furnace/Radiator

➔ A) Hot water for household use

B) Located in forced air ducting

A) 80 gallons if only hot water heater — $3,700. B) For heating house also, use 400 to 1000 gallon tank and more collectors — $15,000.

Diagram 1

TABLE I - HEATING

Types of energy required for each type of heating appliance, the initial cost and the cost per MBTU (million BTU).

Appliance	Energy Source	Initial Cost	Cost per MBTU
Gas furnace	Gas (natural, LP) fuel oil, electricity (for thermostat)	Already owned	$10
Electric furnace	Electricity	Already owned	$24
Stove	Wood or coal	$2,000-$3,000	$6
Solar collector	Sunlight	$15,000	0
Kerosene heater	Kerosene	$100	?

One available model of wood stove is freestanding, with a double-walled chimney. It will comfortably heat a 2,000 sq. ft. home, for an initial cost of $3,000. Other models can be inserted into existing modern gas-log fireplaces. The chimney may require a stainless steel liner to prevent a house fire. To be safe, a professional should be consulted before choosing either option, and a building inspector should check that the installation meets local codes for installation before it is used.

Solar hot water systems are a more expensive investment, and have the added disadvantage of not producing heat on cloudy days. Diagram 1 is a simplified diagram of a solar system to heat household water or even your home. It requires three electric pumps (two are shown, but another that is not shown is required for a heat exchanger). Solar electric panels should be used to power the pumps. As noted, the approximate cost is $15,000.

"Passive" solar heating is often impractical since it must be designed into the house when it is built. Heat pumps also work well in some parts of the U.S.

A kerosene heater requires an open window to prevent carbon monoxide poisoning, which somewhat defeats the effectiveness of the heating.

COOKING

Obviously, an electric or gas stove needs electricity and gas, but a wood-burning stove could be used for cooking at no additional cost while it is being used for heating. Gas grills, Coleman stoves, kerosene stoves, etc., all require a fuel that would need to be purchased unless it had been stored before an outage occurred.

TABLE II - COOKING

The types of energy required for each type of cooking appliance and the cost of installation.

Appliance	Energy Source	Initial Cost
Electric stove	Electricity	Already owned
Gas stove	Gas	Already owned
Wood-burning stove	Wood or coal	(No additional cost if stove is already purchased for heating)
Gas grill	LP gas	$100
Coleman stove	Fuel	$50
Kerosene stove	Kerosene	$85

LIGHTING

Most homes use light bulbs that of course require electricity. Light bulbs can also be powered by solar electric power, wind power or a generator. Without electricity or fuels, solar electric, (also called photovoltaic [PV]), lighting would be the best and safest lighting.

TABLE III - LIGHTING

Appliance	Energy Source	Cost
Electric bulbs	Electricity	Already have
Kerosene lantern	Kerosene	$75
Coleman lantern	Fuel	$75
Candles	Wax	$10/doz.
Solar-powered bulbs	Sunshine	—
Wind-powered bulbs	Wind	—

Numerous other methods of lighting can be used, but some, including lanterns and candles, are dangerous and could result in fires around children and pets. Safety precautions must be taken when using them. Some Coleman lanterns burn as brightly as a 300-watt bulb, while other kerosene lanterns have lower light output and use less fuel.

The last of the four primary areas is **electrical appliances.** They will be addressed in tables in the next section.

ALTERNATIVE SOURCES OF ELECTRIC POWER

Alternative power for each of the needs listed above, as well as for larger appliances, can be supplied by generators, used either exclusively or in combination with other energy sources.

GENERATORS

The most practical alternate source of electrical power is an AC generator. Different sizes are available, from smaller ones that power only some of the appliances in a home to larger ones that will power an entire church.

All generators require fuel. The least expensive generators ($500) use gasoline, while the more expensive ($6,000+) use

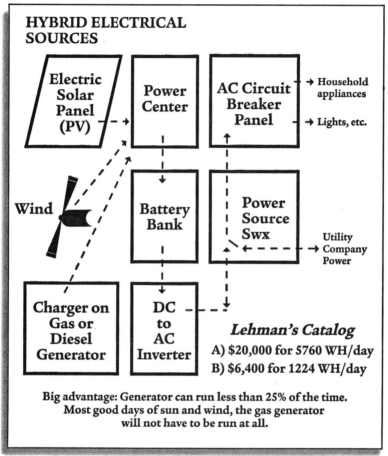

Diagram 2

diesel fuel. Other fuels such as LP gas can also be utilized in many cases.

HYBRID ELECTRICAL SOURCES

In a hybrid electrical source (Diagram 2) the primary source of electrical power is solar electric or "PV" panels. When the sun is shining, the panels provide DC power that charges the batteries through the power center. Of course electricity will not be generated at night, or when the sun is not shining during the day because of storm clouds. However, it is also windy on many cloudy days, so a wind generator can be used to provide DC power to charge the battery. Whether you have sun or wind, the charger on the generator can provide DC power to charge the battery bank.

TABLE IV
HYBRID SOURCES WILL NOT POWER . . .

A hybrid energy system costing $20,000 will not power an entire house. Listed here are appliances that make hybrid power prohibitive because they are high power consumers. Alternative energy sources are suggested for these appliances.

Appliance	Suggested Alternatives
Air conditioning	Fans and iced tea
Electric heating	Wood-burning stove
Electric dryer	Gas dryer or clothes line
Electric stove	Gas, Coleman stove, wood stove
Electric water heater	Solar-powered or wood-burning; Sponge baths
Most lights	Coleman lantern, candles

Before you invest in a wind generator, make sure you have sufficient wind in your area to make it worthwhile. For an hourly reading of wind speeds for cities in the U.S., see the web address in the resources list at the end of this chapter. At the website, you can download a report of recorded hourly wind speeds for several years in hundreds of cities throughout the U.S. For instance, at the Colorado Springs airport, the month of January 1998 had only enough wind needed to run a 5,000-watt generator for two hours. In February 1998, there was enough wind for the equivalent of three hours.

It is best to purchase a package PV system from a reputable company. You can pick the portions of the system you want. For example, you may want everything except the PV panel and wind generator. This would allow you to have power available all day but only run the generator for three or four short periods and not at night.

TABLE V
$20,000 HYBRID WILL POWER . . .

Appliance	Hours per Day	Watt-Hours
Furnace fan	5.0	1,000
Fridge/freezer	5.0	3,000
(Select from the following to total no more than 1,200 watt-hours:)		
Clothes washer	0.8 (one load)	400
Microwave oven	1.0	800
Electric iron	0.5	500
Computer and printer	2.0	1,000
Six 60-watt light bulbs	1.0	360
Television set	2.0	300
Hair dryer	0.5	800
Electric space heater	10.0	15,000 (yes, 15,000)

AC POWER

If there is a power failure, the first line of defense for near-normal household operations in all four primary areas is a generator. However, since electrical appliances use AC power, an inverter is necessary to convert DC power to AC, which in turn can be switched to your circuit breaker panel via a small six-circuit panel.

It is obvious from tables IV and V that the number of appliances and usage time would be limited if using a moderately expensive solar or PV system. Solar power also requires expensive installation. If you are considering using a PV system, refer to the web addresses and booklets listed in the resources list. The last entry in table V is an electric space heater that for 10 hours usage would consume three times the daily capacity of the PV system. This illustrates why you do not want to heat with electrical power, even if you are using a generator.

Manufacturers recommend operating the generator at about 75 percent of its rated capacity. Table VI lists the typical rated powers for some household appliances. Also listed is the starting power required, because the sequence for starting appliances is very important to not exceed the surge power rating of your generator.

In addition to choosing the fuel type for the generator, you will also need to choose whether you want a generator with a manual or an electric starter. You will need an outside enclosure to protect the generator from the weather. Keeping it inside the house is not a good idea when you consider the possibility of fire and carbon monoxide poisoning.

TABLE VI
TYPICAL APPLIANCE POWER REQUIREMENTS

Appliance	Rated Power	Starting Power
Water heater	5,000 watts	5,000 watts
Well pump	1,000	3,000
Fridge/freezer	800	2,400
Furnace fan	600	1,800
Lights (10 60-watt bulbs)	600	600

Hair dryer	1,600	1,600
Electric space heater	1,500	1,500
Microwave oven	700	1,000
Computer and printer	500	500
Battery charger	150	150

Similar to the generator we have just discussed, each of the components in the hybrid system has many features. That is why books or websites should be consulted on each component you are considering purchasing. All installations must comply with codes for safety. The owner and installer must be familiar with the dangers of each component.

ALTERNATIVE COMMUNICATIONS

Normal telephone systems are designed to work in times of power failure. A battery system is utilized that is ordinarily charged by the regular utility power. When this utility power fails, a diesel generator can be used to charge the batteries (Diagram 3). Portable phones will not work without AC power, but a phone connected directly to a wall jack will operate.

If telephone lines are down or the telephone company runs out of fuel for their generators, CB and ham radios are good alternatives. CB radios are cheapest, and do not require a license. However, they have a relatively short range, and undisciplined operators sometimes reduce their effectiveness.

On my way to teach a seminar in Atlanta, I sat next to a ham radio operator on the plane who had served as the sole communications operator in emergency shelters in Georgia during four different emergencies. He explained how he was able to power handheld ham radio equipment with his automobile battery for several days while in a shelter during hurricanes. He said the two- and six-meter ham radios are about the best portable communications equipment for emergencies. These require a theory test but no code test; and there are thousands of repeater facilities around the U.S., giving them an extended range. (See table VII for a summary of ranges, costs and tests required for licenses.)

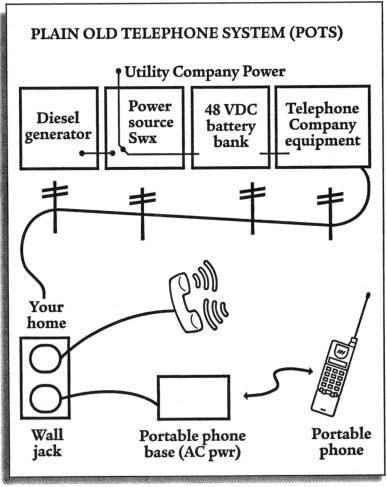

PLAIN OLD TELEPHONE SYSTEM (POTS)

Utility Company Power

| Diesel generator | Power source Swx | 48 VDC battery bank | Telephone Company equipment |

Your home

Wall jack

Portable phone base (AC pwr)

Portable phone

Diagram 3

TABLE VII
CB AND HAM RADIO INFORMATION

Name	Range (miles)	Cost	Code/Theory Test?
Citizen's band (CB)	5-15	$100	No/No
Two-meter FM (handheld)	20-100 in line of sight, more with repeater	$200	No/Yes
Six-meter	20-100 in line of sight, more with repeater	$400	No/Yes
Ten-meter	Local & 100+	$800	Yes/Yes

Ham radio clubs are the best way to get more information. They are listed by zip code at the web address in the resources list.

RESOURCES

BOOKLETS:
1997 Kansas Wind Power. Available by calling 785-364-4407.

Lehman's 1997 Solar Electric Products Catalog. Kidron, OH. Tel. 330-857-5757.

The Solar Electric Independent Home. Available from National Conservation Guild, P.O. Box 3090, Crested Butte, CO 81224.

WORLDWIDE WEB ADDRESSES:
Fireplace efficiency issues—
http://www.penwest.com/legislative/homeown/nar/fireplc.htm.

Gasoline generator safety tips—(also at the above address).

System load worksheet for solar electricity—
(PV)http://www.asis.com/aee/index.cgi?page=catalog/systemloadwrksht.html

Battery sizing worksheet—
http://www.asis.com/aee/index/cgi?page=catalog/batterysizewrksht.html.

Chapter Twelve

Hydroelectric generators, prices and capacity—
http://www.zzzap.com/alt/mircohyd.html.

Specification sheet on Chinadiesel 23kw generator—
http://www.chinadiesel.com/wekw.html.

Hourly readings on wind speed for 400+ U.S. cities for several years—
http://www.nndc.noaa.gov/cgi-bin/nndc/buyOL-001.cgi.

Ham radio clubs, listed by zip codes—
http://www.arrl.org/field/clubsearch.phtml.

HOW THE PLAN HAS WORKED (AND WILL YOU WORK IT?)

The preceding chapters are intended to provide both encouragement and practical how-to sections to help Christians to be "salt and light" in an emergency—spiritually strong, emotionally healthy and intellectually informed with contingency plans.

In this chapter we will share stories from people whose own involvement in disaster relief shows that the concepts of this book actually work. First we will hear from Dale Moseley, who, along with his wife Janell, attended our International Health Services Foundation (IHSF) Disaster Relief Training School and the Spiritual Skills Course in Kuala Lumpur, Malaysia, in September 1997. Dale and Janell then helped install a disaster preparedness plan in Bend, Oregon, and were shortly thereafter able to put into practice what they had learned during a devastating flood in Prineville, Oregon.

Then, because there is wisdom in an "abundance of counselors" (Prov. 24:6, *NASB*), we will also be treated to insights from several pastors around the country who have mobilized their churches to be "lighthouses" for their communities. Next,

Shaunti Feldhahn, founder of the Joseph Project 2000, will share the goals and plans for that ministry. And finally, we will share some insights we have learned from our international experiences as well as our teaching and video conferences. We hope these accounts will spur you on to the good works "which God prepared beforehand" that you should walk in them (Eph. 2:10, *NASB).*

CASE STUDY: THE GREATER LOVE PROJECT IN BEND, OREGON

BY DALE MOSELEY

THE VISION AND THE PLAN

The vision of the Greater Love disaster preparedness project is to train, equip and mobilize teams to provide physical, emotional and spiritual relief to disaster victims. After researching Y2K and its potential effects, I had a desire to help communities prepare for this possible crisis. Neighborhoods of Christians make ideal teams to respond to disasters, including Y2K. Thus came the vision of a neighborhood disaster preparedness model.

It is my desire to see the Body of Christ prepare for and respond to disasters around the world. But how? A vision that my wife, Janell, had is most likely part of the answer. She saw a house engulfed in flames. Disaster relief workers came from all around the world to pour buckets of water on the raging fire. Later in the vision she saw a different scenario, with an indoor sprinkler system already in place before the fire broke out. At the first sign of smoke the sprinkler system put out the fire far before it had lost control. Obviously, preparedness was the wisest choice for the owners of the house. As Proverbs 22:3 says, "A prudent man sees danger and takes refuge, but the simple keep going and suffer for it."

In September 1997, Janell and I attended a two-week course on disaster relief and spiritual skills. This intensive school was put on by International Health Services Foundation in Kuala Lumpur, Malaysia. One of the topics in the school curriculum was the Incident Command System which is implemented in most disasters, usually by the local emergency management agencies (i.e., fire department, American Red Cross, etc.). The purpose of the Command System is to bring order in the midst of chaos, with waves of response under clear and consistent management.

The Command System is the principle that led us to develop a preparedness project for Christians at the grassroots level. Following are the essentials of this plan.

I. Separate the city into sections (use natural boundaries, such as highways, rivers, counties, etc.).
    A. Within each section are multiple neighborhoods.
    B. Within each neighborhood are multiple families.
    C. Identify a chairman and section leaders; neighborhood leaders are put in place as Christians volunteer to help.

II. Seminar on Y2K and disaster relief
    A. Christian radio or other means of awareness and advertising to the Christian community.
    B. Seminar is informative and strategic in an action plan.
        1. Focus on outreach/evangelism.
        2. Alleviate fear.
    C. Individuals volunteer for neighborhood coordinator positions and stay in regular contact with their section leaders.

D. Individuals who are not interested in a coordinator position simply take part in a neighborhood group.

III. Each neighborhood develops a strategy and disaster plan for its area.

   A. Personal household preparation (water and food storage, computer upgrading, etc.).

   B. Communication between families within the neighborhood.

   C. Identify neighborhood resources (wood stoves, generators, wells, etc.).

   D. Identify neighbors with special needs (i.e., elderly, handicapped).

   E. Develop a contingency plan—a list of "what ifs" (power outages, water shut-off, etc.).

IV. Ongoing communication between chairman, section leaders, neighborhood leaders, families, churches and businesses located within the geographic area and non-geographical support organizations (i.e., Red Cross, Salvation Army, power and utility companies, etc.).

WORKING WITH THE MINISTERIAL ALLIANCE

My strategy for Bend was to get as much involvement from local pastors as possible. In the process of inquiring about the monthly Bend Ministerial Association (BMA) meeting, I was informed that there was already a Y2K committee. I contacted the committee chairman, Pastor Dan Dillard, for information about their group. He was excited about my plan and asked me to present it to the BMA the same day, which I did. The following week, I presented the plan to the BMA's Y2K committee, and it was adopted as a working model.

The rest of the project has been carried on by the BMA Y2K

committee, of which I became an active member while I was still in Bend.

We separated the city of Bend into four quadrants, since there are two major highways that run perpendicular through the middle of town. We planned a Y2K community awareness event in four different locations throughout central Oregon. Jack Anderson, of Larry Burkett's Christian Financial Concepts, was invited as a guest speaker. Nearly 1,000 people participated in the seminars throughout the weekend.

The purpose of the Y2K seminar was to give a balanced Christian perspective on Y2K, alleviate fear, encourage evangelism and solicit Christian volunteers for the community preparedness project. As a result of the first seminar, preparedness projects have also been started in Prineville, Redmond, Sisters and Estacada, Oregon.

Three weeks after the initial community awareness event, the Y2K committee held a disaster preparedness seminar. Guest speaker Drew Parkhill from "CBN News" introduced the Y2K issue and gave a workshop on financial issues. Other topics included spiritual preparation, business preparation, family issues, shelter, water and food preparation. About 300 people attended the preparedness event.

Both events were free of charge and cosponsored by the BMA and the local Christian radio station, KNLR. There are no dues or membership fees to participate in the BMA, so funding was limited. A love offering was taken at both events, and contributions covered all expenses, including airfare and honorariums for both speakers, letters and photo-ready bulletin inserts for all Christian fellowships in Central Oregon, and postage. Both events were held in church facilities at no cost. A Y2K information sheet was distributed at the first event, and a disaster preparedness packet was distributed at the second event. The page layout and copying were donated.

As this book is being written, the Bend project is still in process. Neighborhood coordinators are being identified and neighborhoods are preparing interdenominationally for Y2K and other potential disasters. The Body of Christ is functioning as a unit more than it has in the history of the Church in Bend.

(See appendix II for a form that is useful for soliciting neighborhood participation.)

FLOOD DISASTER RELIEF

In the late summer and early fall of 1998, just as Janell returned from Asia, the Red Cross director for Central Oregon called and asked if we would coordinate all humanitarian/religious relief efforts for flood victims in the Prineville district. Many people were homeless. Trailer park homes in particular were severely struck and inundated with mud, requiring us and our rescue workers to use rubber waders.

What an awesome experience this was! Churches and organizations previously closed or uninterested in our vision now began to cooperate. Flood victims are being won to the Lord (great church growth)! Christian rescue personnel were so blessed and fulfilled they are signing up to go to Southeast Asia with us. Glory to God!

COMMUNITY PREPARATION IDEAS FROM AROUND THE COUNTRY

"BACK TO BASICS" IN MICHIGAN

In early 1998, a member of Harbor Light Community Church,

the largest church in the vicinity of Northern Michigan, approached his senior pastor, Bill Mendel, about the potential ramifications of Y2K, the computer millennium bug. Initially Pastor Mendel dismissed the conversation until, during a 40-day fast (part of the "Pray USA" project in early 1998), he was impressed that the Lord was asking him "to be His Body for the community."

Pastor Mendel realized that there were 5,000 people in his rural community who would likely need help during a time of crisis. They had storehouses that needed to be filled, but Pastor Mendel had to reevaluate his definition of a "storehouse." He recalled that Jesus met both physical and spiritual needs. The church became excited about engaging in that kind of ministry.

Church members went to the people and stored up more wood for fuel. They also stored food and looked for ways to expand their food pantries. They started a class called "Back to Basics" that blended practical preparation and biblical principles. They have classes early Sunday morning and Wednesday evening, so people can still attend the church of their choice. In addition, they started "block parties" to build relationships with non-Christians.

Members of the Harbor Light Church are looking at this as an opportunity not to be survivalists but to demonstrate in a practical way God's love by reaching out to their neighbors both with the gospel and with material aid. Their focus is the Lord, but they have purchased much grain and food supplies at no cost for the surrounding churches as well.

PREPARING TO SHARE IN HOUSTON

Rev. Bob Stroud has served as the presiding elder in the Houston House of Prayer, founded by Eddie and Alice Smith. He was one of the people featured on the August 1998 CBN Special on "Y2K and the Church," produced by Chris Mitchell. Bob is a former computer programmer who worked several years ago helping some Fortune 500 companies change the dates on their computers to be compliant after the year 2000.

Rev. Stroud encouraged his fellowship to fast and pray from September to December 1997. The Word the Lord impressed on them was *prepare*. They were to prepare spiritually (in intimacy with the Lord first); they were to prepare for Y2K by "Preparing to Share," and, after waiting upon the Lord, to ask the members of the fellowship to "prayer walk" their community and assess their neighborhoods (ages, disabilities, ethnicities). Then those members of the fellowship who desired to participate were given the option of ordering supplies at a group rate for others in the community. They even moved their meetings closer to the surrounding community by conducting their services in a local park.

"SALT AND LIGHT" IN GEORGIA

Pastor Larry Baker's church in Woodstock, Georgia, a bedroom community in the northern suburbs of Atlanta, has been actively involved in being "salt and light" to their entire community. He has developed and worked with Shaunti Feldhahn, founder of the Joseph Project 2000, offering free office space for her growing needs.

Rev. Baker's younger brother, Dan, the associate pastor, who has served as an Air Force paramedic and chaplain in the reserves, became very concerned about the possible ramifications of Y2K and other possible disruptions in their community. The motto for the church in regard to crises is: "Panic No, Paranoia No, Preparation Yes."

This church has developed a Y2K Task Force and has been

offering free classes on preparation to their community. More people attend these classes in the midweek than usually attend the church on Sundays. Their church is debt-free, has a generator, has planted a garden, and plans are being made to dig a well on the church property.

PREPARATION IN COLORADO

Another example of a church leader mustering his flock to action is Pastor Norm Franz, in Ft. Collins, Colorado. Rev. Franz, who has a strong prophetic leaning, is former president of a finance company. He is sensing a great economic shaking all over the world—a time in which Christians are to be informed with practical and spiritual knowledge to assist those around them who would otherwise never darken a church door if it were not for a disaster in their own lives. His goal is to have a grain and storage facility for many neighborhoods in the Ft. Collins vicinity.

THE JOSEPH PROJECT 2000

The authors encourage you to become acquainted with and consider joining the Joseph Project 2000, founded by Shaunti Feldhahn. Shaunti and her husband Jeff, both Harvard graduates (Shaunti with an MBA and Jeff with a law degree), live in Atlanta. Both are wonderful Christians who are making their lives count for the Lord.

Shaunti worked in the New York Federal Reserve Bank for several years and became integrally involved with international loans and trying to remedy the Y2K problem. She believes that churches should address the current problems, try to be out of debt, and set up a Y2K Task Force that meets every two weeks to discuss issues in the church and community. She encourages the churches to lead community efforts and assess how their communities could be exposed to high risk in a disaster. One of the goals of the Joseph Project is to network cities together.

Other Christian leaders such as David High in Oklahoma City, founder of Millennium Technologies, are pursuing contingency options such as purchasing generators and food at low cost, and food canning machines for emergencies.

WILL YOU STAND IN THE BREACH?

As we close this book, we challenge you with the examples of Jesus Christ and the apostle Paul, who were willing to pour out their lives for others and "most gladly spend and be expended for [the gospel]" (2 Cor. 12:15, *NASB*). Our prayer for you is that your life would be forever impacted by this book! As you choose to be a doer and not just a hearer, we pray that your life's actions and those of the people you raise up around you will help restore the breach of the sin of mankind and the broken-down walls of our lands. God challenges us:

> Is this not the fast which I chose, to loosen the bonds of wickedness, to undo the bands of the yoke, and to let the oppressed go free, and break every yoke? Is it not to divide your bread with the hungry, and bring the homeless poor into the house; when you see the naked, to cover him; and not to hide yourself from your own flesh? . . . And if you give yourself to the hungry, and satisfy the desire of the afflicted, then your light will rise in darkness, and your gloom will become like mid-day. And the Lord will continually guide you, and satisfy your desire in scorched places, and give strength to your bones; and your will be like a watered garden, and like a spring of

water whose waters do not fail. And those from among you will rebuild the ancient ruins; you will raise up the age-old foundations; and you will be called the repairer of the breach, the restorer of the streets in which to dwell (Isa. 58: 6,7,10-12, *NASB*).

May the Lord use you and your spiritual offspring (the "oaks of righteousness"), that you will rise up to be the leaves of the tree for the healing of the nations:

And he showed me a river of the water of life, clear as crystal, coming from the throne of God and of the Lamb, in the middle of its street. And on either side of the river was the tree of life, bearing twelve kinds of fruit, yielding its fruit every month; and the leaves of the tree were for the healing of the nations (Rev. 22:1,2, *NASB*).

RESOURCES

Baker, Pastor Larry. Prayer and Praise Christian Fellowship, 6409 Bells Ferry Rd., Woodstock, GA 30189. Tel. 770-928-2795; fax: 770-924-6935.

Feldhahn, Shaunti. Founder of The Joseph Project 2000, 6409 Bells Ferry Rd., Woodstock, GA 30189-2324. Fax: 770-458-7710; E-mail: jpk@mindspring.com.

Franz, Pastor Norm. "The Elijah Report." Tel. 970-490-1543. Available from http://www.elijahrprt.com or elijahreport@aol.com; INTERNET.

High, David. Millennial Technologies, 8701 N. Bryant, Oklahoma City, OK 73121. Tel. 888-833-0515; fax: 405-467-4352.

Chapter Thirteen

Mendel, Pastor Bill. Harbor Light Community Chapel, 8220
Clayton Rd., Harbor Springs, MI 49740.
Tel. 616-347-5001; fax: 616-347-6310. Available from
http://www.HarborLight.org; INTERNET.

Moseley, Dale and Janell. "Case Study on Community Preparedness." Greater Love, P.O. Box 7196, Bend, OR 97708-
7196. Tel. 541-923-8509; E-mail: grtrlove@teleport.com.

Stroud, Rev. Bob. Houston House of Prayer, 4011 Peppermill,
Houston, TX 77080. E-mail: restroud@ix.netcom.com.

STEPS TO DEVELOP A DISASTER RELIEF/OUTREACH PLAN

MARK NEUENSCHWANDER, M.D.

1. Remember that there is a learning curve consisting of denial, anger, rebellion, unbelief, etc.—a curve that everyone must go through in assessing the reality of an impending crisis and a major change in their lifestyle. Don't become defensive or negative, or allow yourself to become discouraged and filled with self-pity as you seek to involve and inform others.

2. Pray for those you hope to influence, and seek ways to give them practical and timely information from what you have learned in this book.

3. Work with those people now who have an ear to hear what the Holy Spirit is saying at this time.

4. Become actively prepared yourself spiritually by meditating on the verses for your Scripture Storehouse (see Josh. 1:8,9 and chapter 7 and appendix IV of this book).

5. Determine the needs and vulnerabilities of your region, obtainable from your local American Red Cross.

6. God cannot bless ignorance or denial! Ask the Holy Spirit what secular materials you are to read. After

ordering them, develop a quick, practical time line for completion.

7. Assess how many people you could personally be responsible for in your home and fellowship, and for what duration. Then begin to procure the necessary materials to help sustain them.

8. Remember that the more prepared you and your group are with practical plans in place in advance, the greater blessing of peace and provisions you will be to those around you who are suffering hardship and uncertainty.

9. Pray for those in leadership that the Lord wants you to influence with your lifestyle, practical actions and words, whether that be your small fellowship group, neighborhood, colleagues, church or city officials.

10. Assuming that FEMA and Voluntary Relief Organizations are overwhelmed, assess the immediate and possibly long-term needs and potential calamities that your community is liable to suffer in times of hardship—Y2K problems, flooding, hurricanes, tornadoes, earthquakes, potential civil unrest, etc.

11. Become informed about any Christian (i.e., Salvation Army) and secular (i.e., the Red Cross) voluntary organizations that are involved in your community, and what their needs are. Consider taking some on-the-job-training and volunteering with such an organization, so they will know who you are and what you can contribute in times of crisis. (See in chapter 13 how Dale and Janell Moseley, of Greater Love Ministries, and graduates of the IHSF Disaster Relief Schools in Malaysia, assisted the American Red Cross in Bend, Oregon, in disaster relief after a flood.)

12. Find ways to build relationships and be a blessing and assistance to those around you before tragedy happens. A good example is Rock Church in Baltimore, which has neighborhood prayer walks, Adopt-a-Block programs for housing, health and employment opportunities; crisis pregnancy counseling with adoption plans for unwed mothers; a halfway house for those recovering from drug addiction; warehouses for food storage; and two 16-wheeler trucks for food pick-up and distribution.

13. Realizing that community and group preparedness may be essential for the well-being of your loved ones, use your time wisely as a trainer helping to inform and equip the groups you are to reach.

14. You must make hard decisions distinguishing the difference between the "tyranny of the urgent" and those things that are really important. Spend time on the most important.

15. Be willing to invest your time and expertise on a weekly basis in helping your leaders have food, energy essentials (i.e. China Diesel generators), and equipment stockpiled and organized to help the disabled, widows, single-parent families and elderly.

16. Try to liquidate debt as soon as possible, living frugally and saving at least 10 percent of what you earn monthly.

17. Be willing to tithe (10 percent of your gross income) to your spiritual "storehouse" (i.e., your church or where you are fed spiritually). Give an additional 1 percent to a materials storehouse that is procuring the necessary resources for the elderly, disabled and single-parent families.

18. Create a Disaster Evangelism Task Force and guidelines as suggested in chapter 4, surveying your local congregation for members' resources and training. Map out your region and area of influence by determining and developing a Skills Data Base. Look for those who have health-care training, ham radio operators, engineers who know about electricity, safety, plumbing, etc. Find those in your church or community who would be willing to volunteer some of their time and expertise on a part-time basis either to train others or assist in time of great need. Know the best times and ways to contact them. Cornerstone Ministries in Tulsa, Oklahoma, connected with the Seminary and Field Education Department at Oral Roberts University, is developing a prototype program in this regard.

19. Software is now available from Chris Cooper through Mapping Center for Evangelism to help you plot out practical maps and demographics for your city, town or community, if you have access to 911 emergency services in your community. The software is on CD, for $250. Tel. 1-888-MAP-7997; address 8615 Rose Hill Rd., Lenexa, KS 66215. Your church membership can be cross-indexed on these maps if your pastor chooses to become involved. This is a great tool for determining the needs of your immediate community (financial, health, ethnicity, education level) before a crisis occurs and helping you make appropriate contingency plans.

20. Because the Great Commission mandate to every believer is to preach the gospel and make disciples, or "trained ones" (Matt. 16:15-20; Mark 28:18-20), begin to gather easy-to-read Bibles and teaching materials for new

believers (youth and adults) that will equip them and explain the basic doctrines of the Christian faith (see Heb. 6:1,2).

21. Those who desire additional hands-on training in disaster response and developing contingency plans for their communities should consider attending the six-day Disaster Response Training School offered by International Health Services Foundation in Colorado Springs. The program includes a mock disaster and tabletop drills expounding on the Incident Command System. (See chapter 4; and how to contact the IHSF after point No. 23, below.)

22. Those who desire training in spiritual warfare and to be equipped to make disciples who can impact their communities for the Lord should plan to attend the next six-day Spiritual Warfare Institute also conducted in Colorado Springs by IHSF. (See below for how to contact.)

23. Those who are sensing that the Lord wants them to use or develop skills to work internationally in teams with other Christian relief and development organizations or with IHSF, whose thrust is evangelization, church planting, discipleship making and redeeming nations (see Isa. 58:12), should consider attending both six-day intensive IHSF training schools in Colorado Springs.

Contact: International Health Services Foundation
P.O. Box 49536, Colorado Springs, CO 80949-9536.
Tel.: 719-481-1379. Fax: 719-481-1378.
E-mail: ihsf@aol.com.

NEIGHBORHOOD VOLUNTEER APPLICATION

(Mr.) (Mrs.) (Miss) _____

                   (Last Name)   (First)   (Middle)   (Preferred)

Residential address _____

                 (Street)   (City)   (State)   (Zip)

Mailing Address _____

                 (Street)   (City)   (State)   (Zip)

Phone _____ Fax _____ E-mail _____

I am interested in:

❑ Participating in a neighborhood group.
❑ Coordinating a neighborhood group.
❑ Participating on the Ministerial Disaster Preparedness Committee.

What local church/fellowship are you a member of?

_____

What is your pastor/minister's name? _____

Briefly describe your salvation experience.

_____

_____

_____

_____

_____

_____

_____

The answers to the foregoing questions are true and correct to the best of my knowledge. I understand that the Ministerial Association reserves the right to terminate my participation in this effort if any answers are knowingly false.

Signature _____ Date _____

Submit this application to: _____

Action Plan

WHERE DO I GO FROM HERE TO HELP MY CHURCH AND COMMUNITY?

1. Have I become informed by reading this book and studying the areas on personal and community preparedness? Yes__ No__

2. What are the disasters that historically have been of great concern in my region and community, and how were they handled? _____

   _____

   What organizations were involved, and what did they do?

   _____

   _____

   _____

3. What new, potential crises might affect my loved ones, church and community with possible power disruptions, severe economic downturn, natural disasters (earthquakes, hurricanes, tornadoes, partial melting of the polar ice cap, etc.), release of chemical/biological agents by terrorists?

   _____

   _____

4. Who are people I can share this concern with—people "who have an ear to hear," who are doers and not just hearers and who will be able to develop plans to aid those around me?

_____

_____

5. Do I have a basic understanding of the benefits and methodology for setting up a Disaster Response Task Force in my church or community? Yes__ No__

6. Have I made plans to build friendships in my community with non-Christian believers as well as "prayer walk" my neighborhood asking for the salvation of those around me? (See Matt. 18:10; Luke 11:9-10; Rom. 10:13-15; 2 Cor. 4:3,4; 10:3-5.) Yes__ No__

7. What are the strengths, weaknesses and ethnic makeup of my community?

Strengths_____

Weaknesses _____

Ethnic makeup _____

8. Do I understand the advantages of cell groups during times of distress, crises and hardships? Yes __ No __

9. What are these advantages? (Please list):

_____

_____

10. Am I currently involved in an evangelistic cell group?
Yes __ No __

11. Is there a current list of the addresses and phone numbers of people in my church or fellowship with professional or amateur skills that could be called upon in the event of crises? Yes__ No __ If no, what do I need to do to initiate this and share these ideas?

_____

_____

_____

12. How does this assist me in making my contingency plans?

_____

_____

_____

13. Because it normally requires 21 days to form new habits, have I started to begin my scriptural meditation (see chapter 7)? Yes __ No __ If yes, when is the best time of the day for me to do this?

_____

_____

_____

14. Is there a disaster plan for my town, city or community already in place? Yes __ No __ Is that plan available for me to study and know? Yes __ No __

15. After seeking the Lord in prayer, is there any Christian or even secular organization in my area that I'm sensing I am to

volunteer some of my time to, on a regular basis, in order to build relationships and to gain practical experience? List possibilities: _____

_____

_____

_____

16. Are there other things or ideas that the Lord has prompted me about during or after reading this book? (Please list):

_____

_____

_____

_____

MEDITATION AND PRAYER LIST FOR YOUR SCRIPTURE STOREHOUSE

INTRODUCTORY SCRIPTURES

John 15:7	Joshua 1:8,9	Proverbs 23:7	Mark 16:14,18,20
Proverbs 4:20,22	Psalm 1:1-3	Romans 12: 1,2	Hebrews 6:1,2
Isaiah 55:8-12	Jeremiah 17:7,8	Matthew 28:18-20	2 Timothy 2:2

SUNDAY—SALVATION

Matthew 18:3	John 14:6	2 Corinthians 3:16	1 Timothy 2:3,4
John 3:3,5-7	Acts 4:12	2 Corinthians 10:3-5	1 John 5:10-13
John 3:16,17	Jude 1:23	James 5:16b	Romans 1:16
Ecclesiastes 7:20	Mark 8:34,35	Galatians 4:19	Hebrews 1:14
Romans 5:8	Luke 9:23-26	1 John 1:9	Psalm 103:20,21
Romans 6:23	Revelation 3:20	Jude 1:24	Ephesians 2:8,9
2 Corinthians 5:17	Matthew 18:18-20	Romans 10:8-10,13-15	2 Corinthians 4:3,4
2 Corinthians 5:21			

MONDAY—FAITH

Galatians 2:20	James 5:14-16	Jeremiah 17:5,8	Revelation 2:17
1 John 5:14,15	2 Corinthians 4:13	1 John 5:4,5	Revelation 2:26,27
John 15:7	Ephesians 6:16	Mark 11:22-24	Revelation 3:5,6

John 14:12-14	Matthew 8:8-10,13	Jude 1:20	Revelation 3:11-13
James 4:2,3	Matthew 28:18-20	Matthew 17:19,20	Revelation 3:21
Hebrews 11:1,2,6	Mark 16:14-18,20	James 1:2-4	James 2:26
1 John 3:8	Romans 10:8-10	Revelation 2:7	Hebrews 10:38
Proverbs 3:5,6	Revelation 2:11		

TUESDAY—DIVINE HEALING

Isaiah 53:4,5	Acts 8:6,7	Numbers 16:48	Isaiah 61:1-3
Matthew 8:16,17	Hebrews 13:8	Luke 9:1,2	Matthew 14:14
1 Peter 2:24	Mark 16:15-20	James 5:13-16	John 5:19,20
Exodus 15:26	Acts 10:38	Mark 11:22-24	Matthew 4:23
Exodus 23:25	1 John 3:8b	Matthew 8:8	1 John 5:14
Psalm 103:1-5	Matthew 18:18	John 14:1	3 John 1,2
Psalm 107:20	Numbers 23:19	John 14:12-14	Matthew 18:20
Matthew 10:1	John 15:5,7	Matthew 28:18-20	Jude 1:20
Luke 4:18,19			

WEDNESDAY—LOVE, COMPASSION AND FORGIVENESS

Love and Compassion

Matthew 9:35,36	1 John 2:5	James 5:14-16	Ephesians 4:32
Matthew 9:12,13	1 John 2:15	Mark 11:22-24	Colossians 3:12-14
Jeremiah 17:9,10	1 John 2:16,17	Matthew 8:8	1 Thessalonians 5:12,13
1 Corinthians 13:1,4-10	Ephesians 2:4-7	John 14:1,12,14	1 Peter 1:22,23
1 Corinthians 13:13	1 John 4:9-11,19	Luke 4:18,19	1 John 4:7,8
1 Corinthians 14:1	Romans 13:8-10	Matthew 14:14	1 John 3:16,17
Mark 12:28b,31	John 15:5,7,12,13	John 5:19,20	1 John 5:14
Matthew 22:36,40	Romans 12:10,11	Matthew 4:23	3 John 1,2
John 14:21	Galatians 5:13-16	Acts 10:38	

Forgiveness

Proverbs 4:23,24	Matthew 18:32-35	Ephesians 4:31,32	Colossians 1:14
Mark 11:25	Psalm 103:1-5	John 7:24	Daniel 9:9
John 20:23	Luke 23:34	James 2:13	Psalm 32:1
2 Corinthians 5:18	Acts 7:59,60	Romans 2:1	Romans 4:7
Matthew 5:9	Matthew 5:23,24	Matthew 6:14,15	1 John 1:9
Romans 12:14	Luke 6:35-38	Matthew 18:21,22	Colossians 3:12,13
Matthew 18:21,22			

THURSDAY—PROTECTION AND FINANCES

Protection

Jeremiah 17:7-9	Psalm 27:1	Romans 8:2	2 Timothy 1:6,7
Psalm 23	Psalm 4:8	2 Thessalonians 3:3	Psalm 31:2
Psalm 46:1-7,10,11	Psalm 5:12	Revelation 12:11	Psalm 107:2
Proverbs 18:10	Psalm 31:19,20	Psalm 91:5	Psalm 119:133
Psalm 121:7,8	Psalm 97:10	Romans 8:37	Isaiah 41:13
Psalm 84:11,12	Psalm 107:20	Psalm 5:12	Deuteronomy 33:27
Proverbs 3:24-26	Psalm 145:18-20	Psalm 119:116,117	Proverbs 16:17
Psalm 112:7	Proverbs 2:8	Numbers 16:48	Proverbs 28:26
Proverbs 1:33	Proverbs 30:5	Psalm 71:1	Psalm 103:4

Finances

Jeremiah 17:7,8	Proverbs 11:28	Psalm 68:19	Matthew 25:40
Psalm 67:1-7	Proverbs 28:20	Psalm 41:1	Luke 6:38
Deuteronomy 8:18	Proverbs 28:22	Psalm 3:9,10	Matthew 6:33
Deuteronomy 28:1-5	Proverbs 28:27	Proverbs 11:24,25	John 14:13
Deuteronomy 28:8	Psalm 34:9,10	Proverbs 19:17	2 Corinthians 8:9
Deuteronomy 28:11,12	Psalm 37:25	Proverbs 22:9	Philippians 4:6
Proverbs 8:21	Psalm 55:22	Malachi 3:10,11	Philippians 4:19

FRIDAY—WISDOM AND STRENGTH

Wisdom

Acts 10:34	Proverbs 2:6-8	Proverbs 18:4	Ephesians 3:8-10
James 1:5-8	Proverbs 3:1-4	Proverbs 19:8,11	Acts 6:3
James 3:17,18	Isaiah 11:1,2	Psalm 51:6	Ephesians 1:17-19
2 Chronicles 1:9,10	Proverbs 7:4	Proverbs 24:3	Colossians 1:9,10
Daniel 1:8,9	Proverbs 8:1	Ecclesiastes 7:2,19	Revelation 5:12
Daniel 1:17-20	Proverbs 8:12-18	Ecclesiastes 9:18	Psalm 90:16,17
Daniel 2:20-22	Proverbs 8:32-35	1 Corinthians 1:18-30	Ephesians 3:10-12
Proverbs 9:10	Job 12:13	Colossians 2:3	Proverbs 1:5-7
Proverbs 10:13	Colossians 2:4		

Strength

Isaiah 40:28-31	Isaiah 28:5,6	Psalm 37:39	Psalm 92:12-15
2 Chronicles 16:9	Proverbs 24:10	Psalm 46:1-3	Isaiah 64:4
Philippians 4:13	Psalm 92:10		

SATURDAY—ANOINTING AND PEACE

Anointing

Psalm 89:20-23	Acts 10:38	John 14:12,13	Psalm 23:5
James 5:14	Luke 4:18,19	Psalm 133:1,3	Psalm 92:1-4
1 John 2:27	Hebrews 1:9	Matthew 25:3,10	Psalm 92:10,12-15
1 John 2:20	Isaiah 61:1,3		

Peace

Psalm 119:165	Matthew 10:34	Philippians 4:6,7	2 Peter 3:10,11
John 14:27			

Resources for Medical Disaster Planning

Learning Resource Center, National Emergency Training Center
16825 S. Seton Ave.
Emmitsburg, MD 21727
Tel. 800-638-1821
(Request copy of "Off-Campus Loan Procedures")

Grateful Med
Published by the U. S. Dept. of Health and Human Services, Public Health Service, National Institutes of Health and the National Library of Medicine
Available from:
U.S. Dept. of Commerce
National Technical Information Service
52825 Port Royal Rd.
Springfield, VA 22161
or:
MEDLARS Management Service at the National Library of Medicine, Tel. 800-638-8480

Request software packages: #PB92-10544 (IBM PC and compatibles), or #PB889-196083 (Macintosh). $29.95

Pro-Pac
1023 Wappoo Rd., Charleston, SC 29407
Tel. 800-345-3036, 24-hour fax: 803-763-3303
(Disaster relief supplies and delivery)
Teletec Corp.
P. O. Box 20405, Raleigh, NC 27619
(Radio equipment)

The Natural Hazards Data Resources Directory
L. M. Hennig
Natural Hazards Research and Applications Information
Center, IBS #6
University of Colorado
Campus Box 482
Boulder, CO 80309
Tel. 303-492-6819
Fax 303-492-2151
E-mail: tracy_f@cubldr.colorado.edu

U.S. Public Health Service, Centers for Disease Control and Prevention, Emergency Response Branch
Tel. 404-639-0615 (24-hour hotline)

The Command Post and MCI Supply
P. O. Box 193
Milford, OH 45150
Tel. 513-248-0407
(Fire, EMS and hazardous materials command supplies and training materials)

SoftRisk, Inc.
P. O. Box 20163
St. Simons Island, GA 31522-8163
Tel. 912-638-0820
(Emergency/disaster management computer software)

Let Your Light Shine

Walk in the Light

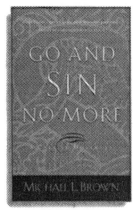

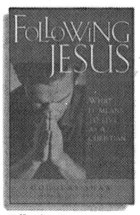